Almost Domesticated

A comedian's collection of essays, short stories, and true tales

By Steve Bjork

D1403309

ALMOST DOMESTICATED
A Comedian's Collection of Short Stories, Essays, and True Tales

Steve Bjork
Wilmington, MA
www.stephenbjork.com
steve@stephenbjork.com

Cover photo by Dick Searfoss
Cover designed by Erik Neilson

TABLE OF CONTENTS

PART TWO: TALES FROM THE ROAD

Foreword

By Steven King

I haven't the slightest idea why I was asked to contribute a foreword for this book, nor am I able to articulate precisely why I agreed.

I have never met Mr. Bjork. Indeed, I've never even heard of him. I received the manuscript, unsolicited, in the mail with a note scribbled in crayon. The note professed Mr. Bjork's great admiration for my work and included a request that I read his book and, if I was so inclined, to write a foreword for it.

I was confused by the request. Why on Earth would I be asked to write a foreword for a collection of *humorous* stories and essays? His entire sales pitch – that we share the same first name – was just ludicrous and simple-minded enough for me to consider.

Sure, I was intrigued. I dug into the manuscript and I must admit that, despite myself, I enjoyed it thoroughly and laughed right out loud many times. It is rather haphazardly assembled with no discernible narrative or theme. He reveals himself to be rank amateur in more than a couple of passages. More than once I questioned his tenuous grip on reality, but all in all I would recommend it for bathroom reading or as a gift to one's less-intelligent friends.

But still, why would he seek me out for a contribution?

Then it hit me.

The imbecile had me confused with Stephen King; author of numerous novels, including "The Shining," "Carrie," "The Stand," and so many others.

To the best of my knowledge, Stephen King, lives somewhere in Maine. I happen to reside in an assisted living facility in central Florida. I was, prior to retirement, technically a writer, which is why I began reading his manuscript at all, I suppose. However, my writing consisted solely of manuals for the assembly of low-end home furnishings. If you ever purchased a bookshelf or a desk at a department store between the years 1983-1997 and assembled it at home, you might be familiar with my work. During the course of my career, if you don't mind my tooting my own horn, I was honored multiple times in the well-respected trade magazine "Manuals, Manuals, Manuals."

Mr. Bjork is apparently not overly concerned with accuracy. I contacted him via telephone about his flagrant error. I explained that Stephen King and I, Steven King, were two entirely different people with startlingly different resumes. We spoke for roughly 10 minutes, all the while he was munching Doritos audibly, which I found extremely rude. According to him, he didn't have the inclination to resume a search for the famous novelist, nor did he have enough extra money to cover the postage of mailing another manuscript. Did I, he asked, have any background in writing – even simple emails? I reluctantly recounted my extensive manual-writing experience, and that led him to beg me to provide a foreword.

"Maybe people won't know the difference, and maybe they'll buy my book based on a foreword that they think is by the famous guy," he said.

So, be warned. Those are the ethics of the author of this collection of humorous essays and short stories.

Will you laugh? Yes, I wholeheartedly believe that you will – often. Should you ever invite Mr. Bjork into your

home? I wholeheartedly believe you should give him a
wide berth.

\-   Steven King (not Stephen King)

Tampa, FL

Introduction

Okay, alright, the foreword wasn't written by the famous author that I had hoped for. Whatever. Still, aside from his snide demeanor, it was a pretty good recommendation. I'll take it!

With all due modesty, I think I can honestly say that what you are holding in your hands is a true work of genius. So you'll be understandably eager to get started. But bear with me here in the intro for a few minutes. There are some things you should know about this fine work of art.

The essays and stories residing within these covers were written over the course of years. Many of them, though certainly not all, were written while I was working as a journalist for a local newspaper based out of my hometown of Wilmington, MA, and were published in a weekly column entitled "The Standing Eight Count." I provide this information because I make reference on several occasions to my position as a journalist and I likewise refer to my long-suffering editor, Shawn Sullivan.

Many of these passages have been sitting in my hard drive just collecting 'dust' for quite some time, which I thought was a shame, since I was proud of so many of them. Others were written much more recently. Each one of them took me long, grueling seconds to create. How could I allow such intensive labor to go unappreciated? I thought it was high time I went through and culled my favorites to share.

My first inclination was to ditch any dated material. I did just that when I felt the references and/or material did not hold up. But, if I felt the material held up to the test of time, I included it. True, the essay entitled "My Dinner With Saddam" can hardly be considered timely at this point, but if you can remember that Saddam Hussein was a fugitive for a short time after the second Gulf War, you'll be able to appreciate the humor. After all, this is not a blog. It's a book. All the material is likely to become dated at some point. Hey, people are still reading the "Canterbury Tales" for some ungodly reason, and that is surely dated - there's not a single mention of Twitter in the entire work.

You should also probably know who I am before you get started. I'm a stand-up comedian based out of Boston. You may already know that. In fact, chances are that you're holding this book solely because you saw one of my shows and were inebriated enough to shell out a few bucks while I was trying to hawk it in the back of the room. I've worked all over the country telling jokes to the masses, and Part Two of the book recollects some of my more interesting experiences on the road.

I sincerely hope you enjoy reading this as much as I've enjoyed writing it. If you read it twice, please send me more money.

\- Steve Bjork
Wilmington, MA

PART ONE: DEMENTED SCRAWLING

Bad Breath

Have you ever found yourself in a conversation with a person whose breath is so bad your knees turn to jelly and you find yourself praying for someone to end your suffering with a merciful lead pipe to the back of your head? That's a rough situation with few opportunities for a graceful exit.

Why is it that Bad Breath People (BBP) always need to tell you something in confidence? It never fails. They do a quick scan of the room and then lean in good and close to tell you a secret. Your ear magically becomes a direct conduit to your olfactory organs, immediately triggering a gag reflex.

"Hey buddy, just back up a step or two and jot it down on a piece of paper, will ya? How many onion and horseradish sandwiches can one person eat in a single day anyway?"

Ever offer a BBP a mint, or a nice refreshing stick of Big Red, only to have them refuse? How are you supposed to react in that sticky situation?

It starts out nice and subtle. You absent mindedly take out a pack of gum and pop a piece in your mouth and then, as nothing more than an afterthought of course, offer the horribly offensive BBP a nice foil-wrapped piece.

"Stick of gum?" you ask nonchalantly.

"No thanks," the idiot replies.

What can you possibly say next?

"Please?"

I have a deep seated fear of having bad breath. Plenty of people seem to be blissfully unaware that their own stank-breath is nasty enough to warrant a quarantine. How do I know that I don't get bad breath from time to time? I do drink a lot of coffee and I smoke my fair share of cigars. Let's face it; there is no market out there for coffee flavored toothpaste, or for cigar flavored mouthwash.

My fear has created a nearly fanatical compulsion regarding my own personal oral hygiene. I am never without mints or gum on my person and I brush my teeth religiously twice a week.

As soon as I become involved in a conversation, especially with a stranger or casual acquaintance, I get the FEAR. Do I have bad breath right now? When was the last time I had a mint? Did he just grimace a little bit when I spoke? Are her eyes beginning to water?

I get so paranoid that I start trying to aim my breath away from their face without actually moving my head. This, no doubt, results in some very odd looking mouth contortions. I've seen smokers do this. Have you ever seen someone smoking a cigarette and conversing with a non-smoker? They look ridiculous in their attempt at nonchalance. They inhale the smoke and, while still maintaining eye contact, they exhale the smoke off to the side or straight down. Can you picture that? Okay, now picture me doing that, but with no smoke.

It is well documented that garlic breath is most unpleasant, but at the very least, that particular pungency can be linked with some sort of food product. The other day I got stuck in close quarters with a guy whose breath smelled like he'd been storing a dead raccoon in his mouth for the last couple of weeks. How else in the world could such a rancid odor be created? It was like fetid underarm odor was coming out of his mouth. How many dentists has he killed during the course of his lifetime?

I was smiling when I first saw him come into the room. He's a good guy and I hadn't seen him for years. My reaction, when first struck by the sledgehammer of stench, was undoubtedly visible, but he seemed not to take notice. Good God, it was all I could do to keep my food down.

It was obvious that he wanted to spend some time catching up and I couldn't see any way out of it. His breath was starting to curl my eyebrows.

I wasn't sure what to do so, as inconspicuously as possible, I just stopped breathing entirely. This turned out to be a very temporary solution. A minute into it he began asking, "Hey, are you okay?" and "Why are you turning all red?" and "Why are your eyes rolling back like that?"

The next thing I knew, he was leaning over me and shaking me awake. There was no need for smelling salts so long as he was around.

"Wow, you just dropped like a ton of bricks," he was telling me, "You sure you're okay? So, like I was saying; when I was in the sixth grade I chose to do my book report on the Bible. Boy, that sure was more than I bargained for..."

I just nodded my agreement. I wasn't hearing much of what he was saying at this point. All of my energies and all of my focus were spent trying to match my exhales with his exhales, and his inhales with my inhales. Inhale. Exhale. Inhale; whoa he's starting to exhale! Switch, quick, switch; exhale. That's was a close one. I got a little bit of a whiff that time.

There I was. Stuck. I was stuck in a corner of a crowded room with a good hearted human being; a person with feelings; a person with hopes and dreams; a person whose heinous breath was birthing disturbingly violent thoughts within my head. It was all I could do to concentrate on timing my breathing and to NOT lash out.

There seemed to be no escape. I was stuck there for days and weeks. I could actually begin to see his breath as it snaked languidly out of his mouth in a mustard-yellowish sort of haze. Some of it would be drawn back into his mouth as he drew oxygen between words, but the majority wrapped itself around my skull, wove itself skillfully through my hair, and then floated upwards to remain hovering mere inches above our heads.

Suddenly a solution appeared. My friend Jeff had foolishly wandered close enough for me to pull him into my personal prison of stink.

"Hey, Jeff. Tom wants to hear the story about when you ate a worm for five bucks," I said.

"Oh yeah?" Jeff responded. He is so proud of that story.

Over he sauntered; pausing with a visible shudder when he hit the Wall-O-Stench. His olfactory organs were attempting an emergency shut-down to battle this horrible affront. He was momentarily paralyzed. This was my chance.

"You're gonna love this story," I told stinky-breath. "I'm just going to go scrub the inside of my nostrils with Brillo pads and then I'm coming right back."

I headed right for the exit. I didn't look back and I didn't feel even a twinge of guilt.

Jeff wasn't doing well. From over my shoulder I could hear him.

"Want a mint?" he asked.

"No thanks," was Tom's reply.

"Please?"

Married Man vs. Supermarket

Well, I found myself in the supermarket again the other day. I don't like it there.

I'm not the regular shopper in my household, but every once in a while I am called upon to help out.

It happens every so often, sporadically and without warning; I should be used to it by now. Like chomping down on the side of your cheek instead of the food in your mouth – you've done it before and you'll do it again, but it still manages to surprise you each and every time.

This last time, it happened just like it always does. There I was, pretending to be busy so as not to be asked to do anything else, when out of nowhere a narrow blue-lined piece of paper, with lots of writing on it, was thrust into my face.

"I need you to grab a few things at the supermarket," my wife told me.

I quickly picked up the hammer lying next to the remote control.

"I'm kind of in the middle of something," I said with confidence. I reluctantly changed my mind. "Ok, honey."

I've learned from experience what every married man should know. Do not argue with your wife about who does more around the house. You will lose.

The next thing I know, I'm cursing and swearing my way down to the supermarket.

Married men are not qualified to be in the supermarket. Just take a look around. At any hour, day or night, you will find no less than eight married men scattered throughout the aisles inspecting food products and confusedly muttering into cell phones.

"Honey? There is Pledge here on the list...do we want our furniture to smell like lemons or potpourri?"

"Hey, you have orange juice here on the list. Do we get pulp or no pulp? ...Yes, I drink orange juice every morning. ...No, I'm not sure whether I chew it or not."

"Hi, Honey. Do we want 85% fat free hamburger, or 90% fat free hamburger? 'Cause I noticed that the 75% fat free is the cheapest and I thought we...hello...? Hello...?"

The best way to get out of grocery shopping is to bring home items that were not on the list; things that will just plain tick her off.

Buy a coconut.

Don't be an amateur – to achieve the desired effect, the coconut must be brought into your home with the appropriate level of fanfare. Be excited about it and refuse to put any of the groceries away until you get it opened. Go ahead and give it a few futile whacks with the ball-peen hammer, and then bring it down to the workshop. Take your time. Start with the hammer and chisel, then move on to the power drill, and finally finish the sucker off with the electric DeWalt miter-saw.

If you time it just right, you will be heading back upstairs with eight fingers and two halves of a coconut just in time to see your wife putting away the last box of Chiparoos (also not on the list). The fact that everyone will consider the coconut milk and meat disgusting just becomes icing on the cake.

I admit coconuts can create a great deal of work in order to get out of a chore, but the supermarket is host to a number of subtler items to choose from. Get creative.

Buy pickled herring.

I can't explain why, but most women hate pickled herring. They seem to be annoyed by herring in general, but if it's pickled they become enraged.

Pickled herring can buy me a good three or four months of no grocery shopping, especially if I make a big deal out of eating a few pieces as soon as I bring it home and then never touch it again. I leave it on the door of the refrigerator so that every time my wife opens it she is greeted by a small clear jar containing chunks of pickled fish flesh, mixed in amongst onions and some sort of cloudy, and partially congealed, brine.

The pickled herring trick doesn't last forever and eventually I find myself back in the supermarket.

I hate going up and down the aisles with my cart. As I am going up an aisle - and I'm traveling in the correct direction - there is a series of people going down that same aisle, and they pass me. No big deal, but as I am going down the next aisle those same people are passing me again. This happens over and over throughout the whole store. Apparently it's just me, but about halfway through the store I feel like I've built up some kind of relationship with these people.

"Hey," I say, instantly realizing my faux pas, but not knowing how to get out of it. "How ya doin'?"

Blank stare, awkward pause.

"How about that spill on aisle five, huh?! I didn't think we'd ever get out of there," I continue undaunted.

Blank stare, awkward pause. There must be some way to get out of this gracefully.

"Remember aisle three?" I ask. "Those were good times."

Blank stare, awkward pause.

"All right then! I guess I'll see you in produce."

Men aren't comfortable in supermarkets. We are okay within the two-foot area they have cordoned off for motor oil and car polish and we don't mind the chip aisle, but there is only one aisle in the store that men feel truly feel at home.

The cereal aisle. As kids, we were all sent to the cereal aisle when our mothers had had enough of us. After jamming the shopping cart into the back of my mother's Achilles tendon for the third or fourth time, and as soon as her wails of pain had subsided, she would always say the same thing.

"Why don't you go pick out some cereal."

I loved those words. Every little boy in America longed to be sent to the cereal aisle. It was the closest thing a supermarket had to a toy department. I'd make my way, knocking over old ladies and fruit displays, anxious to get my hands on a jumbo box of Frosted Flakes, or maybe Cookie Crisp.

There I would be; the cereal aisle would stand towering before me, millions of colorful cereal boxes stacked sky-high. The whole aisle seemed like some perverted supermarket version of the Gardens of Babylon.

Twenty or thirty other little boys were there too, eyes glazed and mouths wide open from sensory overload. Count Chocula, Frankenberry, and Boo-Berry were the best monsters around. The Trix rabbit, Tony the Tiger, Sugar Bear, Captain Crunch, The Froot Loops bird, the Quisp alien dude; the gang was all there. Just once I wanted the opportunity to go hang out at to the Honeycomb Hideout.

Every kid in that aisle knew somewhere deep in his subconscious that there was enough sugar in that one aisle to keep us awake for the rest of our natural lives. Why this stuff was just for breakfast, none of us could fathom.

I still feel at home in the cereal aisle and I'm not the only guy to feel that way. More than once I have seen grown men curled up in the fetal position in front of the Cocoa Pebbles display, moaning something or other about the battery on his cell phone being dead.

Cat Poop and Shame

I think everybody has occasional moments of self-doubt now and then. Moments when you wonder just what exactly has become of your life. It is perfectly normal. I can't say I experience such moments very often, but I had one hit me hard the other day.

I was driving down Main Street and it was an absolutely beautiful day. The windows were open and the radio was on. I had a nice big cup of fresh Dunkin Donuts coffee in one hand while the other gripped the wheel. Plus, I had a Ziploc baggie of fresh cat poop on the passenger seat.

The cat poop was no accident. I had spent the previous 15 minutes sitting cross-legged on the floor outside the litter box with my trusty pooper-scooper in hand while my abnormally shy kitten went about his business.

Bagheera is solid black and was named after the panther from the Jungle Book. He has been living in our house for nearly three months. During his entire residence I have endeavored to retrieve a fresh stool sample for those freaks down at the veterinarian's office.

This task has proven especially difficult since we have two other cats prowling the house – gotta catch him in the act to be sure it's his.

It didn't seem like a big deal at first, I figured that I was bound to see him head into the door of the fully enclosed litter box at some point. He proved to be, however, a true poop-ninja.

At one point, in an act of utter desperation, I locked him in a room for three days with nothing but a litter box, a dish full of Metamucil, a dozen bran muffins, and a bowl of prune juice. Nothing!

Meanwhile, the vet's office has been calling me every week asking if the matter had slipped my mind. I'm sure they were having a great ole' time. I guarantee the whole office gathered around the telephone each and every time for a big laugh.

"Hey everybody, I'm going to call that guy about the cat poop. Shh, quiet! It's ringing. Hello, Mr. Bjork? We haven't seen a stool sample from Bagheera yet. Umm, do you still own the cat? Uh, huh. And you are giving him food?"

"Am I on a speaker phone?"

Our other two cats, Achilles and Kit Kat, were fully aware of my prolonged dilemma and openly mocked me. They'd sneak into the box and make all kinds of digging and scratching noises. To their unending delight, I'd come running down the stairs expectantly just in time to see one of the wrong two cats sauntering out of the box.

So there I was, driving down Main Street with fresh poop; mission accomplished, feeling downright victorious when it struck me – I'm a middle-aged man. And this has all but dominated my thought process for nearly three months.

I really doubt my father ever drove around with cat poop in his car, and I guarantee my grandfather never did. Back in those days, if the cat produced poop at all, it was considered to be a mighty healthy cat. Once it stopped pooping, you went out and got a new cat.

I don't think these three cats are ever going to stop pooping. I am forever scooping their box, and they show up on the scene every single time to supervise the operation and to make sure I do it correctly. They always wear a vague expression of, "What took so long?" and "It's about freakin' time you got around to this."

In my mid-forties and reporting to a trio of cats. That's what it has come down to for me.

I know they don't respect me; that's the worst of it. Every once in a while I'll catch one of them just staring at me and I know exactly what is going through their mind at that moment; "If I was just a little bit bigger I would eat you."

By the time I pulled into the vet's parking lot my mood had completely deteriorated. I picked up the bag-o-poop and shuffled all slope-shouldered into the office and through the crowded waiting room. Men, women, children; they all saw me carrying the poop.

Then, the poop and I had to wait in line. Two people were in front of me dealing with very time consuming non-poop related issues.

Take this advice; if you are going to walk into a veterinarian's office with your pet's poop, bring the pet too. Everybody else has their pets with them. There I was with nothing but a poop in a bag. I just felt like I owed those people some sort of explanation.

"My cat made this," I told one old lady. She pretended not to hear me.

The real salt in the wound, of course, was that after all of that, I had to pay them $20 to take it from me. It's bad enough to openly bring poop into a public place, but then to have to pull out a twenty as well; that is simply cruel and unusual.

I paid with a credit card. Yup - I put Pet Poop Testing on a credit card. The vet very discreetly itemized it as "Laboratory Services."

Y'know what? I don't even think they test it at all. I'm convinced it is nothing more than a big veterinary scam to see how many numbskulls they can convince to bring in animal feces. They get together at annual conventions, compare numbers and giggle their faces off.

I swear I heard that Ziploc bag hit the bottom of the trash barrel as I walked out of the office. And I'm sure I heard hushed giggles.

● ● ●

The North Korea Trip

Shawn P. Sullivan, Editor
Town Crier
104 Lowell Street
Wilmington, MA 01887

Dear Shawn,

I have just received your note informing me that you have chosen not to authorize any expenses incurred during the press trip to North Korea that I recently proposed to you in writing. While I do appreciate the prompt reply, I must admit that I am more than a little baffled in regard to your reasoning.

If I may quote part of your response:

"The Town Crier is primarily interested in news items, features, and stories that directly affect the residents of Wilmington and Tewksbury. Your suggestion that this newspaper should send you (and three guests?!) to North Korea is simply not something the Town Crier is willing to consider at this point. I do, by the way, find it questionable that the flight you have lined up includes a three-week layover in Hawaii before arriving at its ultimate destination of Seoul, South Korea. Furthermore, I find it suspect that you have provided no realistic details as to how you plan to cross the Demarcation Line and make your way up to P'Yongyang in North Korea. Your reference to chartering a river boat and traveling up river in clandestine fashion 'like the dude in Apocalypse Now' was both naïve and foolish.

"I feel compelled to remind you that you were never actually hired by this paper in the first place. We have never actually given you an assignment and have been quite patient with your incessant ranting and raving. Against the advice of our attorney, we have chosen not to bill you for the property damage sustained by the Town Crier building during your most recent unexpected visit. Our receptionist, Ann, has developed an understandable fear of you and has recently begun bringing a handgun to work.

"I hope that I have adequately addressed the major points outlined in your written request, but unfortunately a significant portion of the document was illegible due to a number of, what appear to be, gravy stains. The entire letter, incidentally, reeked of tequila."

After that, Shawn, you become almost completely unintelligible and more than a little belligerent.

I am very surprised that this fine newspaper would take such a short-sighted approach to covering the news and I am offended by your personal attack on me. We are professionals and there was no need for that sort of pettiness.

I have often wondered what it is that motivates your dictatorial persona and I have come to the conclusion that it can be little more than a fear of success. Apparently, somewhere in your subconscious, you don't feel this paper is capable of competing with the Boston Globe or the New York Times.

Well sir, I for one do not concur.

If you are not prepared to play with the big boys, maybe you should pack up your belongings, hop on your mule, and move back up to your hometown of Sanford, Maine. You've accomplished a great deal more than your fellow Mainers ever thought you would. Most of them assumed the ravenous dogs of Massachusetts would pick your feeble bones clean in less than a month, but lo and behold here you are, less than four years later, editor of a weekly newspaper armed with the authority to deny a committed reporter the opportunity of bringing home a Pulitzer Prize for this shabby rag.

I hope you don't stay up on your high horse for very long, my friend. I still remember when you had just come down from Maine and I had to spend a minimum of six hours explaining to you the concept of dental insurance. Even at that I have never been convinced that you more than partially grasp the notion.

I have a number of sources who claim that your departure from Maine was not entirely by choice. I have it on good authority, as a matter of fact, that your marriage to someone outside the family created a sizable scandal.

I am going to bring this letter to an end before I start getting personal, but I will ask you to reconsider your position.

The events transpiring in North Korea are of vital importance to the people of Wilmington and Tewksbury and I have tried to convey that significance to you on more than one occasion by using simple monosyllabic words, but you just don't seem to get it. I can tell you that a number of people, including more than a couple of Wilmington's local officials, have made comments to the effect that they would prefer me to be in North Korea as opposed to the various town meetings.

You should know that I will not hesitate to go over your head if it becomes necessary. I have confidence that your managing editor would side with me on this issue, and would smack you around the office for even hesitating to send me into communist-held territory.

Whatever the outcome, I hope that we can put this trivial bickering aside and continue on as professionals.

Best regards,
Steve

Me and Pepe

I will never forget Pepe.

Pepe was an Irish kid who lived up the street when I was growing up in Wilmington and he was my best friend for many years. I could tell him my deepest secrets, my highest aspirations without fear of being laughed at. He couldn't speak a word of English.

Like most children I had lofty dreams for a thrilling future and I often spoke to Pepe of my dream of someday becoming an insurance salesman. Pepe would always respond with a supportive, "No comprende."

The language barrier never bothered us. We used to sit for hours and laugh at his face.

We started the first grade together at the Woburn Street School and were excited to be in the same classroom. Our teacher's name was Miss Melbatoast and Pepe immediately developed an enormous crush on her. He didn't care that she was seventy-five years old or that she had tragically lost her nose in a freak slide rule accident in the late 1930's.

She broke Pepe's heart, not only by not understanding Spanish, but also by not believing that any such language existed. She promptly put a hockey helmet on his head and insisted that he wear it at all times. Poor Pepe looked so pathetic when she put the helmet on him; just standing there confusedly muttering, "No comprende, no comprende."

It took some time, but Pepe got used to the hockey helmet and so did I. Pepe was a survivor and found many practical uses for his helmet. He found great joy in head-butting small children and pizza delivery men. He became the king of "Red Rover" by running head first into the arms of the opposing team. I always felt safe at recess.

I remember only one bully during our early school days. His name was David, but we didn't like him, so behind his back we used to call him David. He wasn't a very successful bully, actually, as Pepe and I used to beat him up on a regular basis. Nor was he very smart. Every day he would demand our lunch money, but not until after lunch time. Pepe and I would be penniless by the time he asked us for money and he never seemed to understand what he was doing wrong.

After school, as I walked home I would wave at Pepe as he rode by on the little bus.

Pepe would be waiting for me by the time I got home and we would ride our bikes down to Elia's Country Store to buy a can of green beans. We'd sit in the parking lot and greedily eat the beans. Pepe always ate one bean at a time, while I would shove handfuls of beans into my mouth. Pepe saved my life in that parking lot with the Heimlich maneuver. I wasn't choking, but I could very easily have been. I thanked him sincerely for his concern and especially his forethought.

After that incident Pepe would perform the Heimlich maneuver on just about anyone that caught his eye. It was quite a sight to see a seven-year-old child, wearing a hockey helmet, run up to a total stranger and grab from behind, squeezing spastically until the person was forced to cough up something. He was often beat to a pulp as a result of his compulsion, but that didn't bother him because he had just saved a life.

When we were sixteen years old we got our first part-time job at TJ Maxx. I got a job as a mannequin and Pepe worked as a customer service representative. Dissatisfied customers would step up to the counter and scream vociferously at poor Pepe. He would respond with an empathetic, "No comprende."

It was around this time that I noticed a change in Pepe. He became despondent and no longer performed the Heimlich maneuver on anyone. Apparently he was depressed about not being able to speak English.

He dove into his English studies and severely sprained his neck. He was so involved in studying that he didn't have much time for me. We drifted.

When he was eighteen he had reached his goal of graduating the third grade.

With third grade finally under his belt he decided that the school system had taught him all they knew. He quit school and went off into the world to seek his fortune.

I heard about his plans and decided to pay my old friend a visit before he left. When he opened the door and saw me he smiled and gave me the Heimlich maneuver once more for old time's sake. I gave him a pat on the helmet and said goodbye.

That was the last time I saw Pepe, although I think of him often. I also hear stories of him from mutual friends that have run into him on the road over the last fifteen years. Apparently he considers himself an extensive traveler, although he never left our hometown and he never married.

There are times when I really miss Pepe. I can't watch a Boston Bruins hockey game without thinking about him. Sometimes on a calm, silent summer night I'll hear a noise that sounds exactly like someone, unexpectedly, receiving the Heimlich maneuver and I can't help but wonder…is he out there? Could it really be Pepe?

Then it happened.

This afternoon, just a couple of hours ago, I saw him on the street. I was walking down Main Street, when I was suddenly overcome by a strong odor of herring. I immediately became hopeful. I looked and saw his helmet above the heads of the crowd.

As he got closer I could see that his clothes were little more than rags, hopelessly smeared with motor oil, dirt, and God knows what else. It was nice to see that he was taking better care of his appearance.

I was so excited to finally see Pepe again. Where would the conversation start? There was so much I wanted to tell him. My promotion to Head Mannequin. I had choked once. Green beans taste better if they're warmed up.

As he got closer I froze and didn't say anything at all. I just stood there looking at him.

He was almost next to me before he noticed me. He smiled wryly. Then he winked and simply said, "No comprende."

Then he continued on down the street flashing young ladies and laughing maniacally. I couldn't move. I just stood there. Staring at the man named Pepe. I'll never forget him.

My New Mexico Life

I want to buy a tiny little house in the New Mexico desert, just outside of Carlsbad. I want to write drivel all day, undistracted by Internet access, and lie on the gravel at night staring at the star-filled sky.

You've never seen so many stars as from the New Mexico desert. It's as if it's a different sky entirely from the one we are used to in more urban locales. It is the way God wanted us to view his sky. We've ruined his vision throughout most of the country, but it still lives on in New Mexico and western Texas. And probably in northern North Dakota, but who wants to go there?

In New Mexico, I want to be thirsty and dry, with wind-burned, cracked lips. And I would spurn ChapStick.

I would wear shabby clothes and grow a long shaggy beard.

I want to play flashlight-tag at midnight with the sea of jack rabbits that congregate on the Interstate each night.

I want to go into town only rarely for food and supplies, and to let people speculate about the stranger who bought that little hovel on the edge of the desert. "Perhaps you'd like to run for the planning commission or join the Lions Club," they would occasionally say to me. "No," I'll reply enigmatically, "I don't want to do any of those things. I'll just pay for my Pemmican beef jerky and be on my way."

I want to be lonely and unbothered by humankind and I want to make friends with a volleyball.

I want to sleep fitfully on top of the covers in my sagging twin bed in New Mexico from 10:00 a.m. to noon each day. I would listen to the faded wallpaper slowly peeling away from its plaster prison. I would watch the shadow of a solitary housefly languidly buzzing from one end of the pathetic room to the other. And I would consider eating that fly, were it not so skinny from malnutrition.

I want to frequent the area's only bar every afternoon. I would drink cheap draft beer out of a rusted tap, flowing through hoses that haven't been cleaned since the Carter administration. And I would drink bourbon. Oh, yes, I would. Bulleit bourbon would be the only extravagance in my New Mexico life. Aside from, of course, the occasional pickled egg plucked from a glass jar of murky brine sitting on a shelf behind the bar. Pickled eggs, now and again, would fit in nicely with my New Mexico existence.

I want all of those things, on days like today.

My Run for Selectman

With this column, I am officially declaring my candidacy for a seat on the Wilmington Board of Selectmen and I would humbly ask that you cast your vote for Steve Bjork.

I have lived in this town with a great sense of pride for more than 28 years (which, I suppose, would make it 29 years) and now it is my turn, and privilege to raise a family here. While it is true that I spent a couple of years during my twenties living elsewhere, I moved back to Wilmington as soon as the charges were dropped. This town has been good to me and it is time to give something back to the community. I certainly would look forward to serving the people of Wilmington to the very best of my ability, if given the chance.

What, you may ask, does Steve Bjork bring to the table? For one thing, I bring experience in foreign diplomacy. I recently returned from a press trip to North Korea, and while there, was granted a private audience with Kim Jong Il, the sick and twisted leader of North Korea. He laughs every time I describe him as 'sick and twisted.' It has become kind of an inside joke between the two of us and he refers to me as "the capitalist pig-boy." We sure did have some laughs.

I must admit that my diplomatic meetings with Jong were not as successful as I would have liked. I brought my own personal interpreter, who, as it turned out, was not able to speak Korean. Truth be told, he wasn't very proficient in English either, but he was very comfortable with Farsi. Farsi is a fine language, I am sure, but it was of very little help to me on my trip and, regrettably, Jong had my interpreter executed.

Since Jong and I were not able to communicate with words we were left with no other option but to call out for pizza and play Monopoly for two straight days. I'll tell you this; for someone who denounces the institution of capitalism, he was ruthless. He beat me 8 out of 10 times and I'm no slouch.

Jong's Monopoly skills aside; no other candidate for Wilmington Selectman can claim to have experience in foreign diplomacy behind them.

As your duly elected Selectman, I can honestly say that I will bring a strong set of morals and principles to the office. Oh, sure; I can be bought, but only for an extremely large sum of money. I can honestly assert that under no circumstances would my lofty ethics falter for anything less than $250,000 (in small, unmarked bills, of course). ...or maybe for a new Porsche. I have to admit; I really do want one of those.

Aah, but I digress.

I am proud of this town. I come from Wilmington; born and hazed. I am proud to say that I attended the Wilmington public skool system and then went on to flunk out of my first attempt at college.

As my number one priority, I plan to rid Wilmington Center of the filthy rotten muggers and the putrid petty thieves that, at present, swarm the area with impunity. I, for one, still have memories of people walking through the center after dark without worry. This clean-up will not be an easy task, I know, but it can be accomplished by instituting a state of martial law and suspending civil rights on a short term basis. Once all the criminals are rounded up and thrashed to a pulp, I plan to replace them with brand new, and much improved, muggers and petty thieves, at no cost to taxpayers.

This municipality, along with every other town in the Commonwealth, is facing financial difficulties. This town needs a Selectman who will actively seek out and attract new businesses to set up operations here in Wilmington. I am such a candidate. Thanks to my extensive background in corporate America, I have fostered countless connections in many industries, such as bookmaking and loansharking, and I have no doubt that attractive offers can be put together to entice a number of these businesses to town.

This has been a long hard winter and the budget for snow removal has been greatly depleted. As your Selectman, I promise to work hand-in-hand with the Town Manager to ensure that we not spend one red cent on snow removal between the months of May and September.

I have no doubt that I can work well with my fellow Selectmen and Town officials. As a matter of fact, I have spent a great deal of time pestering and annoying many of our fine town officials, and I am sure that through those efforts I have gained a significant level of respect from them. Either respect or revulsion; I tend to confuse those two concepts.

In addition to my promises, I am going to do something that most of the other candidates tend to shy away from. In addition to my campaign promises, I would like to outline a series of campaign threats.

When elected I will go through the voting records and will then instruct the DPW to dig up the shrubs and bushes of every resident who did not cast a vote for me. They may not have time to dig up every bush on each and every property, but are you really willing to take that chance?

Once in office I will keep a running list of people who piss me off and will periodically access the town's computer system to alter their property tax rate. For fun I may just wipe out any and all payments made during the last 20 years. In fact, depending on how the computer system works, and on how badly the person gets on my bad side, I may choose to significantly alter the person's property lines. Maybe I'll just change the zoning of their property to Heavy Industrial. Yeah, that would be fun.

With all of that being said, this year's election is not simply about what the voters want for themselves. No, it goes far beyond that; this year especially. I would like to say to the voters of Wilmington: Stop being so selfish and stop thinking about nothing but yourselves for once. I would ask, respectfully; what is wrong with you freaks? There is a bigger issue on the table this year. Me.

To paraphrase the great John F. Kennedy from his famous inauguration speech in 1960, ask not what Steve Bjork can do for you. Ask what you can do for Steve Bjork. It's high time that the voters of Wilmington realized that Steve Bjork should be elected to the office of Selectman by way of a unanimous vote. In fact; an article should be submitted to the warrant for the next Town Meeting naming Steve Bjork to the new position of Overlord of Wilmington, with complete and total authority over both the town and its citizens.

As your Overlord and Supreme Leader I promise to take good care of you, my underlings. Mark my words: those who supported me will prosper beyond their wildest dreams, while those who opposed me will be forced to work the overnight shift at Simards Roast Beef.

I trust that you will make the right choice on April 19 and I sincerely thank you for your time.

Mike the Headless Chicken

Well, it looks like I won't be making it out to Fruita, Colorado for the big "Mike the Headless Chicken Festival" in May. My wife thinks its "stupid." She thinks it's a waste of time and money and doesn't want me to go. That, as far as I can see, is the biggest drawback to marriage. Compromise. For instance; apparently I am "forbidden" from growing mutton chops. That's right; no mutton chops for me. I discovered that rule quite recently and according to advice from my attorney, I should let it go. He further advises me to consider buying false mutton chops that can be pasted on to my face and then removed whenever necessary. He possesses a brilliant legal mind.

For those of you unfamiliar with Mike the Headless Chicken, allow me to enlighten you. I have been made aware, incidentally, that I have been accused of stretching the truth from time to time. I assure you that everything in this column relative to Mike the Headless Chicken is true and can be verified at www.miketheheadlesschicken.org or by checking the calendar of events at www.fruita.org, the official homepage of Fruita, Colorado.

In September of 1945, Clara Olsen sent her husband Lloyd Olsen out to the chicken coop to pick out a nice bird for the family's evening meal. She sounds really bossy. It could probably be assumed that Lloyd was, like me, forbidden from growing mutton chops.

At any rate; back in the 1940's there were no Market Baskets or Shaws close to the Olsen's farmstead in Colorado and they were apparently forced to do really disgusting things in order to eat. Lloyd grabbed the closest rooster along with his trusty ax and took care of business.

It is true that chickens will run around for a few seconds after decapitation before realizing that they are, in fact, dead and should probably stop all the fuss and just go ahead and lie down, but Mike was no ordinary chicken.

Yes, Mike ran around the yard like a chicken with his head cut off, because that is exactly what he was, but as the initial shock of the situation wore off he chose not to settle down and die. Lloyd waited patiently for the ceremonious dance to end, but as he glanced up from his watch he noticed that Mike had gone back to mingling with the other chickens, sans head of course.

Apparently, Lloyd was a very difficult man to impress. According to the account posted on the official website, "Lloyd left Mike to figure it out for himself and didn't see him again until the next morning." There is no mention of what Lloyd and Clara had for dinner or whether he had mentioned this oddity to his wife at all. As far as I know, Lloyd grabbed the next closest chicken and lopped his head off with much more success.

Lloyd was a practical man and when he found Mike the next morning, sleeping with his unattached head (**unattached head!**) under one wing, Lloyd decided that, "Goshdarnitt, if that bird wants to live this badly I am going to help it."

I assume that is what Lloyd said according to the tone of the story, but if I happened to see a headless bird snoring happily and hanging on to its skull-piece like it was the Headless Horseman from Sleepy Hollow, I'd be doing an impromptu load of whites in the washing machine and calling on the church to exorcise the devil from my chicken coop.

But not good ole' Lloyd. He picked up the closest eyedropper and began feeding Mike water and grain through his esophagus. According to the story, it was right about now that Lloyd realized Mike was "special."

Scientists at the University of Utah determined that he (by he, I am referring to Mike, not Lloyd) had retained one ear and enough of his brain stem after the "ax incident" to allow him to function quite well. The ax blade had missed his jugular and a well-placed blood clot kept him from bleeding to death.

Mike lived for 18 months without a head and acclimated well, though he admittedly never did quite as well with the female chickens as he once had. He continued to strut around the yard, pecking at the ground and preening at his feathers. Mike grew from 2.5 pounds at the time of his decapitation, to nearly 8 pounds.

Lloyd didn't need an ax to chop off *his* head to see a good thing. He started traveling the country with "The Headless Wonder Chicken," charging happy rednecks $.25 for a peek at Mike. Mike also received a spread in Time Magazine and Life Magazine. Mike declined a nude, though fairly artistic, lay out for Playgirl.

Tragedy struck while the Olsens were in a motel in the Arizona desert. Lloyd and Clara were awakened in the middle of the night by the sound of Mike choking. Lloyd was unable to find the eye dropper in time to clear Mike's throat and he passed on. Lloyd and Clara helplessly watched their winning lottery ticket slump over, and things were never the same for them.

Rumors persist that Mike's demise was not quite what the fine people in Fruita would have you believe. Unnamed sources have indicated that Mike got carried away with his new found fame and that he didn't have enough of a head on his shoulders to be able to handle it. Some say that Mike went way out of control, drinking tear-droppers full of booze and eating handfuls of "magic" corn. More than one hen has publicly admitted to a sordid affair, and literally hundreds of chickens all over the country have claimed to be illegitimate descendants. The "official" cause of death may have been due to choking, but few in the know believe it.

The spirit of Mike lives on in the third weekend of May in Fruita, Colorado during the Mike The Headless Chicken Festival. Events include chicken dancing and a pet parade in which people dress their pets to look like chickens. That one is a big favorite amongst the pets. There are, of course, the "Run like a chicken with its head cut off 5k and 10k races"

People visit Fruita from all over the world for the festival. Maybe I'll get to go next year. And maybe I'll grow mutton chops just for the occasion.

My Dinner With Saddam

I hate the "Drop in" visit.

I should qualify that general statement. I don't mind when someone drops by because they have extra tomatoes in their garden and they would like me to take some off their hands. Or maybe they bought too many steaks and they would never be able to eat them all. Yeah, the steak thing never happens; but keep me in mind if you ever find yourself in that predicament.

The visits that I dislike generally involve a second-tier friend who just happened to be in the neighborhood and figured they should stop by. They don't bring tomatoes or even beer, but they do expect you to be completely free for the rest of eternity to entertain them.

Just give me a call first. Give me the opportunity to make up some lame excuse. We'll both know it's a sham, but it saves time for both parties. I can come up with a lie on the phone, but once I see someone standing at my door I immediately become a sap and can't turn anyone away.

I suppose that's why I felt so put out when Saddam Hussein showed up at my door unannounced.

I had been up for most of the previous night writing a theatrical musical based on the contamination of soil at the Olin Chemical site in Wilmington. The working title is, "Unlined Lagoons and Waste Water." I'm not exactly married to that title, but it tends to sum up the general feel of the music and lyrics.

My doorbell rang unexpectedly at the crack of 10:00 a.m. on a Tuesday. I hadn't showered yet and I couldn't imagine who would be ringing my doorbell at such an ungodly hour.

I opened the door to find Saddam standing on my front steps, fidgeting nervously about and glancing back and forth from side to side. The whole world was looking for him, and there he was on my front steps. He was smiling at me as he walked right in. Uninvited, I might add.

I had never met Saddam, but apparently Kim Jong II, the sick and twisted leader of North Korea, suggested he look me up if he was ever in this area. He said he was hoping to be able to crash for a couple of days.

Not wanting to come by empty handed, he handed me a canned ham as he made his way past me and took off his coat. I tried to be congenial, but found it difficult to initiate small talk while he went through my house checking in all the closets and under all the beds. He finally relaxed a little bit when he was convinced the house was clear, but he did make a rather bizarre comment about the need for civilians in case things "get rough." Then the jerk made a bee-line for my fridge. What a nerve on that guy.

He cracked open a beer and made his way downstairs. I couldn't help but wonder how long I was going to have to entertain this freak. Man, I hate surprise visits. My hopes for a quick visit were quickly dashed when he paused at the sliding glass doors and looked out into the backyard.

"Oh, good, you have a pool. That's gonna be great when it warms up some," he said as he slipped over to my recliner.

The man possesses no manners whatsoever. He told me recliners are "tacky" while he yanked on the handle and leaned back. Then he kicked off his smelly shoes, turned on the TV and asked what kind of snacks were in the house.

I don't care how tacky he thinks recliners are. I like to put my feet up and relax when I watch television. Saddam was definitely starting to get under my skin.

The rest of the morning, and a good portion of the afternoon for that matter, were spent watching television, playing cribbage and putting a sizable dent in my beer supplies.

My wife was none too happy to see our guest when she came home and she wasted no time calling me upstairs for a summit.

"How long is this loser going to be staying here?" she demanded. "I don't like him and I don't trust him. How do you know he doesn't plan on inviting some of his terrorist buddies over here?"

"Look," I told her, "I don't like him either, but the last thing we need is to upset him and have thousands of Islamic extremists declaring a jihad on the infidels on Kendall Street. He and I had a long talk. We set up some ground rules and established several agreeable resolutions. We even have them numbered; so what can go wrong? If he doesn't keep his word, on the street he goes."

"What if he breaks one of your resolutions? How much leeway are you going to give him?" my wife pressed.

"I'm not going to give him any slack; and I am going to keep a close eye on him. I don't trust him either, but has agreed to inspections and he does seem to be cooperating so far."

"Well, he's your responsibility. I am constantly putting up with your immature friends and those comedian buddies of yours that crash here for weeks at a time; and I never complain. The last thing I need in this house is a maniacal Arab dictator. I better not see even one of his dirty socks lying around on the floor," she told me.

"Former dictator," I reminded her. "Don't worry. I got it covered."

"I have pork roast planned for dinner tonight," she told me. "If he doesn't like pork he is out of luck. I'm not cooking anything else."

I grabbed a fresh bag of Doritos and headed down to see Saddam reading the local paper.

He put up his hands in anticipation for the Doritos and I tossed them over to him.

I am a collector of boxing memorabilia. One of my most prized possessions happens to be a boxing glove signed by Muhammad Ali. I keep it in a display case right below a 16" x 20" signed photograph of Ali and Joe Frazier.

I noticed the display case was empty. I also noticed that Hussein's ratty duffle bag had been moved right next to his chair.

"Where's the Ali glove?"

"What are you talking about?" Saddam asked incredulously.

"I believe that you have my signed Ali glove in your duffle bag," I told him calmly. I am, after all, a fairly patient man.

"I do not have any Ali glove in my duffle bag and you have no proof to the contrary."

"Listen, stupid," I said as calmly as I could. "I am giving you twelve minutes to admit that you have my glove and not a minute more."

"You are just looking for a reason to fight me. It is you that is the aggressor, not me. You want to search my bag?!"

He grabbed his bag and started rifling through it as I towered over him infuriated.

"Okay, look," he said, "I admit; I did take two of your DVD's." He pulled out The Godfather and Pulp Fiction and handed them to me.

"You have my glove too."

"I have no glove. Why don't you present proof of this allegation? There is no compelling evidence!" Saddam challenged.

"If I don't have my glove in 5 minutes, I am going to pull out every hair of your mustache one at a time."

"You are a warmonger," he screamed. "You are just looking for a reason to attack me. Okay, okay. I took your sterling silver salt and pepper shakers too, but that is it, I swear."

"Time's up," I told him.

He looked around quickly for a human shield, but it was too late. I hit him hard and fast with precision strikes about the head and shoulders. He began to cry and tried to slap back with both hands in a childish windmill type of move.

Enough was enough. It was time to end this.

I grabbed the can of mace that I keep on my DVD shelves, for just such an occasion, and gave him a nice healthy 15-second dousing at close range. He let out an ear-piercing high pitched scream and slumped to the ground rubbing his eyes and gasping for breath.

"How does it feel?!" I demanded. "How do you like being gassed by someone that you thought should protect you?"

He had assumed the fetal position and was sobbing like a school girl. I gave him a couple of good solid boots to the ribs before picking him up by his belt and dragging him out of my house. I tossed him into the street and a gang of kids playing street hockey recognized him. They chased him down the street and that was the last I saw of him. Who would have thought a guy with a belly like his could run like he did?

"I hate drop-in visits," I muttered to myself as I headed back in the house.

I didn't find my Ali glove right away. It took some time and effort, but eventually I found the glove tucked away in a secret compartment of his duffle.

I never doubted that he had it.

Mulletts

Yes, I had a mullet.

We all did, don't even try to deny it. It was the 80's and if you were a male between the ages of 14 to 35, and not serving in the U.S. military, you most likely sported a hairstyle falling into the mullet variety.

For those uninitiated in the ways of the mullet; a mullet is a distinctive haircut with a relatively short, clean-cut appearance in the front, on the sides and on top, but with significantly more length in the back.

Mullets can be categorized in a number of different ways. Business in the front; party in the back, for instance. My next door neighbor describes mullets as 10/90's; as in 10% of the hair is in the front and 90% of the hair is in the back.

One devout follower of the Church of the Devine Mullet once told me that he kept his hair the same way he kept his lawn.

"Nice and neat in front and out of control in the back," he told me. He was a nice guy, but who did he think he was kidding. He doesn't have a lawn. I'm quite sure he lives in the constant fear that someone is going to come along and slash the tires on his house.

There are a number of mullet variations floating around out there and the gentleman that I just described sported the epitome of the Trailer Park Mullet (TPM). Unfortunately, many of those unfamiliar with the wide variety consider the TPM as the premiere example of mulletness. The TPM involves a whiffle-cut on the sides with a long straight mullet hanging down the back. The top of a TPM is usually of medium length with a spiked look, but can often have a Shaun Cassidy-like part in the middle with accompanying "feathering" effects. If you are interested in seeing some prime examples of the TPM, just watch a few episodes of the television show "Cops." They generally adhere to a strict "five-mullet minimum" rule for each episode.

It should be noted that the Trailer Park Mullet has never been in style, not even in the 80's.

There is also, of course, the Seinfeld Mullet. Many don't even remember that Jerry walked around with a mullet, but check out the weekday reruns. In the early seasons, Jerry exemplified true mulletude. He sported the most common form, and most widely accepted mullet, which basically consisted of a normal haircut, with some length in the back.

I am tired of hearing people, in the same age bracket as me, denying that they ever had a mullet. Some of these idiots still have one and don't even know it.

Not sure if you had one? Here is a quick test. Did the back of your hair come down past your gold chain (another shameful item that every guy had in the 80's)? If it did, and trust me it did, you had a mullet.

Go ahead and pull out the pictures. Somewhere up in the attic or down in the basement is a picture of you with your black Reebok high-tops and pegged jeans with your mullet head poking out from your Ocean Pacific shirt. Maybe the best picture has you and your mullet standing on the beach in a cool pair of Jams along with that sweatshirt you cut the arms and neck out of.

Or maybe you were more of a Z Cavaricci puffy-pants type of guy, with those pointed gray dancing shoes. The mullet looked good on the dance floor of the Palace in Saugus, didn't it?

Men don't have a corner market on mullets. Female mullets do exist and are usually accessorized by a flannel shirt.

There is no shame in admitting to your past life of mulletdom. Everyone was doing it. Take a look at the television of the time. Tony Danza, Kirk Cameron, Michael J Fox; they all had mullets. Movies too. If Luke Skywalker and Han Solo could have mullets, how could it not be cool?

Mel Gibson sported the Ulti-Mullet in the first Lethal Weapon in 1984, but is was steadily trimmed down as the character became more and more stable until Mel went completely mulletless in Lethal Weapon 4.

It becomes uncomfortable, however, when you run into a mullet-adorned head nowadays.

I went to a Quiet Riot concert several years ago with a couple of friends and it was one of the funniest nights of my life. The band was up on stage wearing the exact same spandex outfits they wore in their 80's videos and the audience was little more than a sea of angry head-banging mullets in their mid-thirties.

Were these freaks really that out of touch with acceptable styles or was it some kind of sad protest. Perhaps these people had some measure of success in the 80's; whether true success or perceived success is irrelevant. Maybe they were the stud of the fast food restaurant they at worked in 1985 and so they never left. As they drive to work every day in their 1987 Chevy Monte Carlo, with the red bandanna hanging from the rear view mirror and the Playboy door locks, they are wondering why it has become so difficult to get a date. Having no other explanation, they simply blame it on the fact that their pain in the neck parents still live at home.

I saw a mullet walking down my street the other day and I prayed to God that he hadn't bought a house in the neighborhood. It is common knowledge to those in the real estate business that a mulletous homeowner can decrease neighboring property values by more than $50,000.

Any child seen with a mullet warrants an immediate phone call to the Department of Social Services. If that is not a subtle form of child abuse, I don't know what is.

Despite everything written so far, mullets do have some positive attributes. The next time you are called upon to speak in public, instead of picturing everyone in their underwear, which is customarily suggested to alleviate feelings of anxiety, picture the audience with mullets. How could you possibly be intimidated by an audience of Mullet Monsters?

That technique can also be used in reverse. During a long meeting go ahead and imagine the speaker with a mullet. You'll be able to sit through the most excruciating insurance seminar with a smile on your face.

Father's Day

Ten was a difficult age for me.

I found out, around Christmas time, that there was no Santa Claus. I was emotionally crushed. The great man that my parents had told me about was nothing but a dirty lie. I walked around as nothing more than a shell of a child. My innocence had been lost forever.

On Christmas morning, I woke up slowly, trudged down the stairs and into the living room where stood our Christmas tree surrounded by, what looked like, hundreds of presents. I realized then that I didn't care whether Santa existed or not; as long as I got my loot.

I lost a tooth in February. I was very excited because I knew that there would be money involved. The Tooth Fairy would be coming. The kid who punched my tooth out told me that there was no such thing as a Tooth Fairy. Once again my parents had perpetuated a lie, but I made a tidy profit and didn't raise much of a stink.

The next bombshell hit in April when I found out that the Easter Bunny was also nothing more than a fictitious character. Again, I was depressed, but I got my chocolate eggs.

All of these traumas occurred in a matter of months, but the worst was yet to come.

The final straw came in June.

I started crying violently and uncontrollably when my mother told me Father's Day was coming up.

We got through it, although they maintained that the man posing as my father truly is my dad. I still have my doubts from time to time.

Let's face it; parents are not perfect people. I guess the most glaring shortcoming of most parents would be their inconsistencies.

Take, for instance, potty training.

I remember potty training quite vividly. If I returned from a successful trip to the bathroom I was showered with praise and affection. My mother proclaimed me to be a "good boy" and soon I would be able to wear "big boy pants" all the time; or so I was told.

My father beamed with pride each and every time. He felt a strong sense of serenity and comfort knowing that he had such a competent son to carry on the Bjork name. There was nothing we could not accomplish.

Life was good. All was right with the world.

I'm an adult now and I don't live with my parents anymore, but sometimes I call them to share a recent bathroom success story. When I do this, however, their reaction is usually one of confusion, almost disappointment, and very seldom are they complimentary.

I am a parent myself, a father to be specific, and luckily for my son; I have perfected the parenting process for his unending benefit.

My son has no idea how lucky he is to live in the world of today. Just look at his video games. He has the newest Playstation and X-Box; upgrades, by the way, from the Nintendo 64 and obsolete Playstation that have been discarded to the back corner of his closet for fear that one of his friends might think he actually still uses them. The characters in these games are more realistic than I am. Sometimes I am convinced that I can actually smell their breath.

When I was a kid I had Atari 2600, which was state-of-the-art gaming at the time. The "controls" consisted of a joystick bigger than your head with one big orange button. My favorite game was "Adventure" and the main character was a cube that wandered aimlessly around the screen looking for these ink-blot-looking-things, which were supposed to represent dragons, to fight. I distinctly remember being duly impressed with the graphics.

I own a snow blower to ease in the removal of snow from my driveway. The only person experiencing ease is my young son for whom the snow blower is far too dangerous to operate.

When I was a kid we only had one tool for snow removal and no matter how hard I tried, I was unable to locate a single dangerous moving part on the shovel.

Don't worry; my son is getting very close to the acceptable age for operating heavy machinery. I swear to God, my father had me mowing the lawn when I was five.

There was no end to the menial tasks I was instructed to perform. Channel changing on the television was a primary function of my existence. The only conceivable way for my father to channel surf in those primitive days was to set up a chair for me right next the huge 26" console television. In fact, my father told me recently that if they had invented remote controls sooner I'd never have been born at all.

My son is a great kid, but you have to stay one step ahead of them and keep them on their toes all the time.

One of the most important concepts to instill within a child is the essential sanctity of life. They must be made to understand that every moment that they do not seize and cherish is a moment wasted never to return. There must be a million ways to instill such a lesson within your children and different methods work for different children. For instance, at least once a week I enter his bedroom during the night dressed up as the Frankenstein monster and I stand next to his bed until he wakes up and sees me. At the instant of eye contact I lunge toward him with my arms raised over my head while making that "eeee-eeee-eeee-eeee" sound from Psycho. Did you see Psycho? Still holds up to this day as a very scary movie. Check it out when you have a chance.

* * *

Anyway, my son screams a little, and I chuckle a little; you know, just to let him know that everything is okay. I take off the Frankenstein mask and spend a significant amount of time consoling him. We usually share a couple of Lifesavers and a couple of laughs.

Sure, it seems a bit elaborate, but I know that he truly appreciates life each and every time. He is never late for school; I can assure you of that.

That reminds me, I need to return that phone call to the Department of Social Services.

Weddings

Well, it's wedding season again.

This is the time of the year when seemingly normal people consider it a sound financial decision to spend tens of thousands of dollars on the events of a single day. These same people will generally start planning for the big event up to a year ahead of time, but it doesn't much matter. Two weeks before the actual wedding all of their longstanding plans will completely crumble for no good reason and will have to be completely reorganized anyway.

I had very little input on my own wedding and I wouldn't have had it any other way. I nodded politely when shown swatches of material for bridesmaid's dresses. Up until that time I had no idea that a "swatch" was anything other than a cheap plastic watch made popular during the 80's; a period of time, by way of association, that also embraced the mullet.

I showed up at the tux shop that my wife picked out when I was supposed to, and then I picked my tux up at that same location a day before the wedding. My part was done.

The only detail I took a stand on was the cake. The cake my wife picked out was priced at nearly $1,000.

A cake.

$1,000.

Why would a cake cost $1,000? No one at the Yum Yum shop has ever tried to stiff me for $1,000 worth of birthday cake. Ahh, but it's not a birthday cake; it's a wedding cake. Put the word "wedding" in front of any product and watch the price skyrocket. It's disgusting.

There was no way that I was going to spend $1,000 on a crummy cake that no one was ever going to remember. Have you ever heard anyone comment on the cake after a wedding? I don't know what kind of freakshows you hang around with, but I haven't.

"Hey, how was the wedding?"

"It was great. You wouldn't believe the cake they had! It was like angels came down from heaven and baked them a cake better than any cake that has ever existed on this Earth. I had two pieces and then I smeared a third piece all over my body."

No. You never hear that.

"Hey, how was the wedding?"

"It was great; open bar all night. I don't remember much of it and I was a little bit cloudy for about three days."

Yeah, that's the kind of thing you hear.

Anyway; I refused to pay $1,000 for a cake; and all of the other "more reasonably priced" wedding cakes were grossly overpriced too. Finally, I decided on pie.

Pie was a great idea and once I set my mind on it I couldn't be swayed. True, blueberry might not have been the best choice. I probably should have gone with apple. Hindsight, as they say, is 20/20.

The wedding gown was also grossly overpriced, though I was never given an exact dollar figure on that item. All I know for sure is that it is somewhere up in the attic packed away in a box supposedly protecting it from air, water, dust, and nuclear fallout. Come to think of it; I have no way of knowing for sure that the dress is really in that box. We gave the dry cleaners a dress and they gave us back a sealed box. Sounds like the biggest racket existing in the dry cleaning business to me.

My wife and I honeymooned in Malden. We stayed on the Saugus side of Malden of course. There is so much more to see and do in that area.

My sister, Karin, got married recently.

She has been living in Austin, Texas for the last several years, at the insistence of the State of Massachusetts, but she got married up here.

My sister and I have always been close, but I don't get to see her as much as I'd like to because her career as a professional mechanical-bull rider keeps her very busy. That's a tough business and she is rated as one of the top 10 professional mechanical-bull riders in the entire country.

Her new husband seems like a good guy. He was born and raised in Texas and he says, "y'all" a lot, but he's okay.

People in Texas are always "fixin" to do things.

Instead of saying, "I'm going to punch you right in the face," a Texan says, "I'm fixin' to punch y'all right in the face, ya stupid yankee."

Texans will say, "Are you fixin' to put some pants on before going to the store?" instead of saying, "Are you going to put some pants on before going to the store?"

My sister has managed to pick up the Texas expressions, but hasn't lost any of her Boston accent.

It is rather disturbing to hear her say things like, "Y'all are wicked pissa," and, "I'm fixin' to go down to Mahhket Basket."

At any rate, they had a beautiful ceremony. I wanted to be the ring bearer, but my sister was afraid I would lose the rings. The ring bearer job was split between my two 3-year old twin nephews, Sean and Kellan. Yes, they were cute, but I don't think I'll ever be able to completely forgive them.

I next lobbied for the position of flower girl, but my beautiful 5-year old niece Cayman ended up landing that job. My family is so uptight.

I ended up being an usher. Whatever.

As the other ushers and I were dragging the bridegroom, kicking and screaming, into the church, I could tell that he wasn't really fighting as hard as he could have been. The medication began to take effect and he stood in the right place at the right time and repeated the words he was supposed to repeat.

My sister walked up the steps and then up the aisle without falling down or doing anything else really cool that could win $10,000 on America's Funniest Home Videos. Something like that can really make a wedding worthwhile.

With my sister down in Texas, my mother had done most of the organizational work for the big day and she was stressed to say the least. When the minister asked if anyone would speak out against the wedding my mother turned to the crowd and flashed a 44-magnum handgun. I guess that might have been a bit uncalled for.

The reception continued into the wee hours of the night and it was a great time. They didn't take my advice about the pie, but it was a great time anyway.

Ingenious Carnival Ideas

My hometown of Wilmington prides itself on its Fourth of July festivities, and well it should. Thousands of people come out to enjoy the weeklong celebration. Hundreds of volunteers dedicate their precious time on our nation's birthday to provide food fun and thrills to the entire community. The carnival is a huge draw, pulling people in from surrounding communities. From horseshoes and water balloon tosses to whiffle ball and basketball tournaments; there is something for everyone every single year. The hospital bed race is one of the highlights and the popularity of the event has even prompted some talk within the international community of including it as an official event in the next Olympics.

It has long been my dream to contribute in some way to the festivities. I had a couple of great ideas for carnival booths, not unlike the ever popular dunk tank, but my ideas were mercilessly shot down by the Wilmington Fourth of July Committee. What do they know about fun?

My first booth was a good old fashioned knife-throwing booth. Wilmington does not presently have one.

I have it all ready to go. I painted a silhouette of a human body onto a 4'x 8' piece of plywood and propped it up with a couple of 2"x 4"s.

Who didn't want to be a knife thrower when they were a kid? Well, now the general public can finally have an opportunity to try their hand at it. Just two bucks buys anyone the chance to hurl three big razor-sharp carving knives at their best friend. Then, for another two bucks, he/she gets to take a turn throwing at you.

I even supply the knives.

● ● ●

I know what you are saying; sounds like fun, but how can I win a prize? Easy; after the third knife has been thrown I measure how close the thrower was able to get to his/her friend without hitting. If all three knives are within, oh, an inch-and-a-half maybe, you would win a really big pencil. Prizes could be traded in for bigger and bigger prizes all the way up to the really super giant pencil measuring nearly 8-feet tall. People love winning big pencils at the carnival.

If you hit your friend, no prize! In fact, you may even have to spend some quality time with the Chief of Police, which adds a little bit of excitement to the whole thing.

"But Steve," you say, "what if my friend is too chicken to stand still while I throw knives at him/her?"

Not to worry. I would have several bottles of Tequila on hand for nervous-Nelly-types. If Tequila doesn't work, I have a full staff of homeless people ready to step in when needed.

But wait, there's more. This is not just a two-person-at-a-time booth. There will be a betting table accommodating up to 24 four people betting on the outcome of each throw. Those people would be encouraged to drink Tequila too.

I spoke to someone at Wilmington's Fourth of July Committee about it, but it didn't go over very well. He must have been having a really bad day, because the more I tried to explain it the more upset he seemed to be getting. Maybe he had had a similar idea and was mad at himself for not acting on it. Whatever the reason for his anger, he didn't need to take it out on me.

He kept saying things like, "That's not safe," and "People cannot drink alcohol at the booths!" and "What the hell did you say your name was?!"

So much for that one.

My next idea for a booth was inspired by the age old "Guess How Many Jelly Beans," or whatever that stupid game is called. You know; the game where there is this great big glass jar full of jelly beans and you have to guess how many jelly beans are in there and the person who guesses closest, without going over, wins an oven mitt or something like that.

I like to think that I have greatly improved on the concept.

The booth I have built is called, "Guess How Many Leeches."

Stick with me on this. It takes some explaining, but it is worth it.

I start with an ordinary see-through dunk tank and I add 5,000 live leeches to the water. Good start, right? Luckily for me, my good friend, Pepe, owns and operates a leech farm, so I can get them cheap.

One at a time, at various times throughout the day, I have various Town Officials, publicly elected Officials, and well-liked community figures suspended above the water of the tank by a harness. The "participant" hangs suspended like that for a half-hour or so to build up an interest level and some suspense from the crowd. The participant would be encouraged to call people over and to act like a typical carnival barker.

Once a sizable crowd has gathered the good natured participant is lowered into the tank up to his/her neck and the water is agitated until the leeches are good and angry.

After being submersed for precisely five minutes, the participant is again lifted out of the water and I would personally count how many leeches have managed to attach themselves to the good sport.

I know what you are saying; sounds like fun, but how can I win a prize? Onlookers are encouraged to guess how many leeches will end up being stuck to the participant for a buck a guess. All bets must be placed before submersion begins. The closest guess, without going over, wins a big pencil.

• • •

For volunteering, the participant gets a big pencil too, which will come in handy when filling out the forms at Wilmington's Family Health Center. Leeches can be pretty stubborn sometimes.

Once again, I called the Fourth of July Committee and spoke to the same grumpy Independence Day Scrooge.

He got all upset again and said, "We can't allow that!" and "That's disgusting!" and "The police are tracing this call and they know who you are!"

That guy has got real problems.

I didn't bother to call back with my idea for a "Be William Tell" booth even though I had already purchased two dozen bushels of apples and more than fifty arrows.

I'm really disappointed about the whole thing. I just wanted to help. I just wanted to contribute. Can I help it if I have some great carnival oriented ideas?

What am I going to do with all of these stupid big pencils?

Day of the Pizza

Will any of us ever forget the terrible ordeal of the Pizza? It was so many years ago, but I remember it like it was yesterday.

I happened to be in Boston on that fateful day and was walking down Boylston Street when I noticed a large crowd gathered in front of an electronics store window. The crowd, however, turned out not to be watching the TV's. Their attention was focused on a street performer eating shoe polish for tips.

It was during his intermission that our attention was drawn to the televisions.

We received the story in scraps and pieces at first. This was, of course, because it was sweeps week and also because "suspense is fun," as Ted Koppel kept telling us.

In the interest of time and space I'll unfold the full story as we eventually learned it from the National Enquirer.

The villains of the story, as everyone now knows, were the Symbionese Liberation Navy (SLN). Not to be confused with the Symbionese Liberation Army (SLA); the revolutionaries who kidnapped Patty Hearst in the 1970's. The SLN was more despicable, more bloodthirsty, and had more body odor than the SLA.

On August 3, 1993 the SLN kidnapped a pizza. An innocent extra cheese and pepperoni pizza.

The SLN contacted the media, via Federal Express, with their one demand. The Pizza would be released coinciding with the release from prison of Tony "Three Nostril" Mancini, the alleged leader of the SLN.

If the SLN's demand was not met, they would mail the Pizza back to the pizza parlor...one slice at a time.

They included in the package one pepperoni slice. The authorities brought in an Italian to identify the meaty substance and he concluded that it was, in fact, a pepperoni from the missing Pizza.

He also concluded that the pepperoni had been removed from the Pizza with a pair of pliers.

America was shocked and disgusted. The SLN had proven beyond any doubt that they would stop at nothing to further their cause. Their cause, it was later discovered, was a bridge group that met once a week. Tony Mancini represented the crucial fourth and without him, the group would be unable to play.

The entire country seemed to rally around the cause. The condition of the Pizza seemed to be the only thing people wanted to talk about. People would approach complete strangers.

"Oh, that poor Pizza," they would lament.

"I know! I pray every night for that pitiful Pizza," would be the general sentiment of reply.

The Pizza was kidnapped from "Pizza Up The Wazoo," which was located on Commonwealth Avenue right across from Boston University. Don't look for it today, it no longer exists, but back then the owner seemed to be on the eleven o'clock news every night crying and pleading with the pie's captors.

"Please don't hurt my Pizza! I'll do anything you want, just don't hurt him!"

The Boston Police leapt into action and got some doughnuts. "This is a job for the FBI," their spokesperson told the press.

The FBI followed suit and got their own doughnuts, which were much nicer with many containing jelly, and others being frosted.

The sentiment of the general public was that not enough was being done in an effort to secure the safe release of the Pizza. America wanted the Pizza freed no matter what the cost. Colorful slogans began to appear on bridges, billboards, dentist's offices, television, and even on the living room walls of single parents. Many popular phrases were coined on behalf of the hapless Pizza. "Free the Pizza" was very popular.

You couldn't pass a single college campus or tractor trailer school in America without hearing shouts of, "The Pizza wants to go home!"

Many celebrities turned their full attention to the issue and one result of this was, as many will remember, the mega concert; Pizza Aid. Van Halen headlined the event and all proceeds went to the Coalition of the Pizza.

There was also the tremendously successful comedy benefit put together by Billy Crystal, Robin Williams, and Whoopi Goldberg; aptly named Pizza Relief.

Meanwhile the authorities suffered setback after setback in their investigation.

The investigation was being headed up by Special Agent, Harvey Wallbanger. He had become stumped very early on and the SLN didn't seem to leave him any clues.

On a hunch, Wallbanger showed up at Pizza Up The Wazoo and asked the clerk if the Pizza had been a pick-up or delivery. Wallbanger had brilliantly deduced that if it was delivered, the customer would have given an address. With an address it might be possible to find the SLN; very possibly in thirty minutes or less.

The Pizza had been picked up.

That destroyed Wallbanger's theory. He became so despondent that he immediately shot the clerk.

The SLN were starting to feel invincible and again they contacted the media, this time adding to their demands an autographed picture of Ed Asner. The letter ended ominously with, "We're getting hungry."

An autographed picture from Mr. Asner was obviously out of the question. Special Agent Wallbanger felt renewed pressure to solve the case as quickly as possible.

• • •

Two nights later, as his wife was shaving his back, Wallbanger came up with the answer.

The very next morning he went to Pizza Up The Wazoo. Wallbanger approached the new clerk in Pizza Up The Wazoo and asked for the procedure involved in ordering a pizza for pick-up. This time his hunch paid off. Every customer was required to leave a working telephone number for verification of the order.

Wallbanger looked up the phone number given for the Pizza and called. No one was home, but the outgoing message on the answering machine said, "Thanks for calling the SLN at 15 Tyne Daly Boulevard in Boston. We're not in right now, but leave a message and we'll get back to you as soon as possible."

What a break! That was the same exact address that appeared on the personalized stationary used for both ransom notes. The SLN had made a tragic error. Wallbanger was so happy that he immediately shot the clerk.

Wallbanger left a clever message on the machine which would lead the SLN into a trap and would ultimately solve the case. The next day the three members of the SLN marched themselves into the police station.

"We are the SLN and we have come to claim our free toaster," they told the police dispatcher.

They were subsequently charged with many crimes, none of which were specified to the defendants or to the public. When asked about this, the public defender representing the SLN was quoted as saying, "Oh, who really cares what the charges are. They're guilty as sin anyway."

The ensuing trial lasted for nearly thirty grueling minutes.

The jury found the SLN guilty on all charges. The judge sentenced them all to three hundred years in a maximum security prison without health insurance, but suspended the sentence if the defendants agreed to mow his lawn every other week. The media and general public were satisfied by the verdict and sentence.

The Pizza was recovered safely and returned to Pizza Up The Wazzoo during a huge welcome home reception and media circus. It was a wonderful time for everyone. There was drinking in the streets and true brotherly love between all. Good had triumphed over evil and the world was ecstatic.

Then someone noticed that the Pizza was covered with mold.

The Pizza was thrown away and everyone went home, not quite as happy as they were a moment ago, but certainly a little wiser in the ways of the world.

Scratch Tickets

I can't stop in the convenience store for a bottle of juice anymore. It's just not worth it. Every single time, I get stuck behind 20 or 30 unshaven addicts spending their entire lifesavings on scratch tickets and lottery. It's never a quick transaction; especially if they come in with a winning ticket. Instead of taking the cash and being happy, they end up blowing the whole thing on more tickets like they are ordering a dozen donuts.

"You won a hundred bucks; congratulations," the clerk tells the wide-eyed gentleman wearing a trench coat and no pants.

"Yeah, right. Give me two Lucky 7's, one Snake Eye's, three Busted's, five Life Loser's, one Scratch N' Sniff For Dollars, two Deuces High's, umm, aaah…"

"You still have $45 left."

"Y'know what; let's make it four Lucky 7's, six Snake Eyes, keep three Busted's, four Life Loser's, eight Scratch N' Sniff For Dollars, three Deuces High's, and how about two Crossed By A Black Cats."

"You still have $14 left."

Okay, let's play the Daily Numbers with that. 3491 is the number and I want $2 to come out exact, $3 any order, $1 first three numbers, $1 last three numbers, $2 middle two numbers, $2 for my home address to win, and $2 for numbers   I'm   not   able   to   count   up   to."

"You have $1 left."

"Gimme a Snickers."

By this time my apple juice has had time to go through the entire fermentation process and I end up getting pulled over by the police on the way home for having an open container of alcohol in the car.

It goes much quicker when they buy their tickets the way most of us buy gas.

"Give me $50 worth."

Everyone wants to win the Lottery. Even I want to win the lottery and I don't play. I have enough vices without spending my hard earned cash on a zillion to one chance.

"Somebody's gotta win," they say just before hitting you up for a $10 loan to cover the cost of some groceries.

That's true, somebody does have to win. But it turns out not to be you week after week.

There is nothing wrong with occasional scratch tickets for fun or even playing one of the big weekly games every week, but come on; draw a line at some point. I know some people who are convinced that if they buy more Mass Millions tickets, they can't help but win.

"I bought 20 tickets for Mass Millions this week...y'know; to increase my odds."

Congratulations; you've improved your odds from one in a zillion to 20 in a zillion. You would still have a better chance of being struck by lightning while wearing a rubber suit and crouching under a sofa in your basement.

So, what would you do if you won? Everyone has that discussion from time to time and I have yet to meet someone that doesn't have the whole thing planned out.

"I can tell you one thing," most people tell me, "I wouldn't be going back to work! What is up with these people that still go to work every day?"

Interestingly enough, many of the people who give me that speech don't even have a job in the first place.

I worked for several years in a very conservative, suit and tie, environment and I can tell you, most assuredly, that I would be at work the day after winning the lottery. In fact, I would be the first one there. I would have a cigar in one hand and a bottle of Bulleit bourbon in the other. I would sit there as happy as can be and just do my work as if nothing had happened. What a great day that would be. Work can actually be a lot of fun when you're not worried about losing your job.

I would definitely have the boss's car towed to some impound lot in a bad section of Boston.

At some point during the day I would put on a ski mask and streak through the office.

I would go into the refrigerator just before noon and eat all of my co-workers' lunches. I would vehemently deny it even though my waste basket would be overflowing with brown paper bags and various Gladware containers.

I would sneak up to the reception desk whenever possible answering the phones as, "Steve's Pizza and Methadone Clinic."

Basically, if I got away with all of that I would continue reporting punctually to the office everyday with ill-fitting suits accompanied by clashing ties and sneakers. I would produce substandard levels of performance until they had no choice but to fire me and then I would go ahead and collect unemployment.

Hopefully by that point I would have used up all my sick days and vacation time.

Tip Cup Insanity

Is there anybody out there without a Tip Cup?

Why are we suddenly tipping all kinds of people that were never before considered tip-worthy? Why am I expected to tip the Dunkin' Donuts people? I'm never asked to tip the fine folks at McDonalds.

Don't get me wrong. I am not against the general concept of tipping for services rendered. I understand, and fully support, the concept of tipping waiters and waitresses; especially the ones at Hooters.

If anything, I over-tip for a sit down meal, but I do take issue with that obnoxious question that every waiter or waitress on the face of the Earth will unfailingly ask whenever you pay the check with cash. They come over to the table, pick up the cash without counting it, give you a big ole' smile and ask loud enough for every surrounding table to hear, "Would you like me to bring you back the change?"

This question is naturally designed to shame you into shrugging the idea off as ridiculous.

"No, I'm all set," you are supposed to answer with a nonchalant wave, "The total came to $21.68 and the smallest bill I had was a $50, but I want you to have all the change. Here, take my watch too."

Luckily for me, I am not easily shamed. The following conversation takes place each and every time.

"Would you like me to bring you back the change?"

"Yes, I would," I say with equal volume. "That's how this works, you see. If I pay you with anything but the exact amount I was charged, then you bring me back all of the change. Then, and only then, I will go ahead and make a decision about how much of a gratuity I want to leave for the service you have provided."

You want to be careful about the exact timing of that sort of dissertation, by the way. You don't want to become overzealous and deliver that speech before the dessert arrives or you may unknowingly end up eating a nice parfait glass full of Ex-Lax Mousse...or worse. Never mind how I know; just trust me on this one.

Unfortunately, the entire concept of a "tip" has been grotesquely transmogrified by our society over the last couple of years. According to the dictionary; a tip is, "a small sum of money given to someone for performing a service; a gratuity." Check the dictionary again in five years to see the word's definition evolve into, "a generous sum of money given for very little service whenever a Tip Cup is present and the cashier holds your change just long enough to make you feel uncomfortable about accepting it."

I remember when each Dunkin' Donuts had a counter, complete with stools and waitress service. Back then they used ceramic coffee mugs and dishes to serve their customers. I remember it like it was yesterday. I was about 5 or 6 and my mother would take me to Dunkin' Donuts after every hockey practice. It is a memory that I think back on fondly.

For some reason I always wanted to be perceived by the other patrons as a grown-up when I sat at that counter. I would sit up good and tall, smoke cigarettes and pretend that my hot chocolate was a coffee. Only grown-ups are allowed to drink coffee.

Meanwhile, my mother would pretend that she hadn't just poured three of four ounces of whiskey into her coffee.

Boy did she drink a lot of coffee during those afternoons. Back then, Dunkin' Donuts had signs all over the place saying, "No tipping Please." As the afternoon rolled on I would watch my mother leaning back and forth until finally she would just tip right off the stool and I would be so embarrassed thinking those signs were put up just for her.

I often wonder what happened to those signs.

There is no more sit down counter service at Dunkin' Donuts. They have become donut slingers for hire. Today they give you a coffee in a Styrofoam cup, toss a couple of donuts in a bag and shove the Tip Cup in your face.

But why do I tip someone who makes my coffee wrong 6 times out of 10 and then shoves it through a drive-thru window at me? If they want a tip I should be allowed to stay at the window while I enjoy my coffee along with periodic refills.

Whenever I walk up to the counter of a Dunkin' Donuts and see the Styrofoam cup with handwritten scribble reading "TIPS" I pick it up and spit into it. Oh sure, people are shocked and angry at first, but I settle them down before any punches are thrown by innocently explaining that I am dyslexic and thought the cup had an entirely different purpose. At that point, of course, I turn the whole thing around by accusing them of discriminating against dyslexics and then I threaten to sue.

It's not the twenty-odd cents that I take issue with, by the way; I think I can spare it. My issue is with what Constitutional lawyers call the "Slippery Slope." The concept of the Slippery Slope is often used to argue against allowing small and insignificant violations of our Civil Rights because they can hypothetically set the stage for greater and greater infringements down the road. As a trite example; if they were to ban the sale of automatic weapons, what would stop them from eventually banning the sale of all weapons; yes, even slingshots.

Following the logic of the slippery slope, if we offer encouragement of the Tip Cup at Dunkin' Donuts now, where will we see the next Tip Cup and where, oh God where, will it end? You can forget about whether or not we will see Tip Cups in the rest of the fast food establishments; that has already become sickeningly inevitable.

But where will it stop?

Will there be a Tip Cup in the muffler shop? The hospital emergency room? Will your secretary have a Tip Cup on her desk? Will police present you with a Tip Cup after issuing you a citation?

I can definitely see a Tip Cup replacing the "Take a penny, Leave a Penny" dish in the convenience store. Why not? Someone had to stock the shelves with grossly overpriced snacks.

Following the Slippery Slope to its forgone conclusion; eventually everyone will walk around with Tip Cups hanging around their necks like jewelry and everyone will just tip each other all day and no service will be provided to anyone at any time.

Well, I for one do not intend to miss out on this Tip Cup racket. If you happen to visit my home, you will see a five-gallon water jug sitting on the floor just inside the door. That's mine. Be generous and no spitting, please.

My Own Newspaper

I think newspapers are on the cusp of making a huge comeback. This whole Internet thing is just a fad. That's why I'm working towards launching a newspaper for my hometown of Wilmington.

I have a dream.

In my dream I am the owner of an obscenely successful newspaper and I'm up to my neck in cash. I have a huge mansion with an indoor swimming pool the size of a lake; but without the urine, of course. In fact, I have two pools; one for swimming in and the other to rinse off afterwards. Donald Trump is calling to borrow a ten-spot and Don King is asking me to bankroll a fight between Mike Tyson and Kim Jong Il, the sick and twisted leader of North Korea.

I have high hopes for my new publication, which will go under the very original name of "The Town Yeller."

I have countless innovative ideas that I can't wait to institute.

News is easy when things are happening, but the real trick is filling up the white spaces when nothing is going on. That's why; when I get started on my new paper I am going to feel free to make stuff up when things get slow.

I will have the traditional police log in my newspaper. My twist is that, although I will report on the actual police activities, I'm also going to spice it up a little bit.

Each week I will pick out several people randomly from the phone book to appear in amongst the arrest logs along with rather embarrassing charges. Those lucky individuals will be notified one hour before the paper goes to print. All they have to do is answer their phone or call the paper back before the ink hits the page and, for a very reasonable contribution, their names will be removed. The size of the contribution will be dictated by me and will be set, on a sliding scale, in relation to the embarrassment factor of the charge to be listed. Lewd and lascivious, for instance, should fetch a pretty penny.

It's very similar to one of those radio contests. I think people will like it.

Also; headlines in my newspaper will have nothing at all to do with the actual story.

Readers tend to scan the headlines, but only read the story if the topic interests them. Somebody took the time to write that boring story and, dammit, people should read it. That's why all of my headlines will be "grabbers."

"Wilmington Votes to Invade Burlington and Seize Water Supply"

You'd read that one wouldn't you? Especially if the little headline below it read:

"Town Manager Says Burlington Is Full Of Godless Heathen!"

Then you start reading the article and it is about some guy who collects belly-button lint or something like that. You'd end up reading the whole article and forgetting what got you started.

As a marketing technique, I will have young boys dressed in 1930's type clothes on every corner selling my paper. They will scream, "Extra, extra! Read all about it!" even though the paper will only come out once a week.

I'm a visionary. Been that way all my life.

Bjork's Fall Foliage Extravaganza

Welcome to autumn in New England.

Right now, as we go about our daily lives unsuspecting, hundreds of Bluebird and Peter Pan buses are making their way up Route 95 determined to get to New England just in time for peak foliage. The leaf peepers are coming.

That's right; this is the time of year when seemingly normal people from such exotic locales as South Carolina and New Jersey come up by the busload to view the beautiful foliage in New England.

I'm not sure exactly when "foliage" became so prevalent a word in the New England vernacular. When I was a kid we used to call them leaves. Nowadays; up in the tree = foliage. On the ground = leaves. To translate further; up in the tree = beautiful. Covering my entire yard = tremendous pain in the butt.

I found one travel agency on the Internet advertising a Fall Foliage trip leaving from New York City for the low, low price of $2,200. That trip lasts 7 days, which averages out to roughly $314 a day to peep at leaves.

What a rip off. I smell opportunity. I have recently applied for a tax ID number for my newest endeavor, "Bjork's Fall Foliage Extravaganza." Naturally my tour has a "hook" in order to significantly differentiate it from the competition.

Allow me to explain.

Who wants to be stuck on a tour bus for hours upon hours looking at the stunning array of colors in faraway trees while every muscle is allowed to atrophy into something resembling, if not tasting like, lime jello?

Not you, that's who.

Would you want to go to a mountain and watch people ski all day? Of course you wouldn't. You would want to get into the action, you would want to ski. You would want to feel the freezing wind in your face and the powder under your skis. You would want to lose feeling in your extremities while your nose runs incessantly down your upper lip.

Well then I ask you, who wants to look at foliage in faraway trees?

People who don't know any better, that's who.

Bjork's Fall Foliage Extravaganza is different. It puts you right smack dab in the middle of my backyard and right into the heart of the action. It's kind of like the world's first foliage theme park.

We provide you, our valued customer, with an opportunity to actually wade through foliage piled as high as your knees.

Listen to it rustle beneath your feet. Go ahead; reach down and pick some foliage up. We encourage it. Feel it in your hand. Rub it on your face if you want to. Breathe in the fresh scent of newly forming molds. We don't mind.

Bjork's Fall Foliage Extravaganza is the only tour available that allows you to enjoy the spectacular fall foliage with all five senses. That's right, all five senses. If you're peculiar enough to want to taste it, then more power to ya, buddy. We will not judge.

No other foliage tours allow such hedonistic indulgences.

Do the other tours include a free rake?

No, they do not.

Do the other tours allow you to take home free samples of authentic New England fall foliage?

No, they do not.

Sign up with Bjork's Fall Foliage Extravaganza today. The super low price of $250 per day ($249 for senior citizens) includes, an authentic New England "Leaf-rake" just like the pioneers of the 1980's used, a slice of pumpkin bread bought from a genuine New England store (Market Basket), accommodations for sleeping under the stars in and amongst bona fide New England foliage, and an endless supply of honest to goodness New England leaf-bags to cart away as much complimentary foliage as your little heart desires.

Foliage makes excellent Christmas and Chanukah gifts for friends and family, so don't be shy; take as much as you want.

Sounds great, you say?

It sure does, but wait. There's more.

All of those other low-rent foliage tours leave (no pun intended) out one of the most important aspects of autumn.

Acorns.

Sign up with us before October 15th and we'll throw in as many real New England acorns as your suitcase and pants pockets can handle.

Acorns have hundreds of uses. Whip them at small children passing by your house. Use them as chips at your next Texas Hold 'Em poker night.

"I see your acorn and raise you three acorns,"

Sounds exciting doesn't it?

But wait! That's not all.

The first 25 callers will receive a cookbook entitled "101 Acorn Recipes." That's right, from Acorn Pot Pie, to Stuffed Acorns, to Crème of Acorn Soup, this cookbook has them all.

Operators are standing by.

The World of the Supernatural

I have recently become intrigued by the world of the supernatural. Unexplained phenomena occur every day all over the globe. With a little bit of research, I have found a share of strange and bewildering occurrences.

Take, for instance, a story recently documented in which a man accidentally hit his thumb with a hammer and his twin brother, who was watching television in a neighboring town, screamed in pain at that very instant. That man's thumb was soon covered with a black and blue mark while the first man suffered no pain at all.

A week later, those two twin brothers, Jim M. and Joe M., got into a heated argument. In a fit of rage, Jim M. began smashing all of his own fingers with a hammer, causing Joe M. to experience excruciating pain. Jim M. was subsequently arrested for assault and battery to himself with a dangerous weapon.

That story became especially eerie when it was discovered that the brothers were not identical twins, nor even fraternal twins, but were in fact Irish twins.

Just this week a man reportedly offered indisputable evidence of his ability to read minds. Unfortunately, this gentleman is capable only of reading the minds of infants. Since these infants are not yet able to speak or understand English the gentleman is merely able to discern vague desires for nourishment, and comfort.

Last year a senior citizen named Alfred A. gained national recognition for his uncanny ability to communicate with his deceased wife. Alfred's wife of more than 40 years passed away nearly two years before, but Alfred showed evidence that he is still able to communicate with her at will in a "Crossing Over with John Edwards" kind of way.

In an interesting twist, Alfred refuses to use his amazing gift, claiming that this is the first peace and quiet he has had in more than 40 years and that he has no intention of letting her, "mess this up."

Then there is Jeff L. who has a fairly similar situation. In Jeff's case, an apparition of his deceased mother appears before him at least twice a week, although luckily never while he is in the shower. According to Jeff, he has no control of when or where she will appear, but it generally occurs when his bed is not made or when the house needs a good dusting.

Jeff's mother will often stay for dinner, but doesn't eat much and spends most of her time criticizing his wife's cooking and then leaves halfway through the meal.

Don't forget about Mark R. who suffered a near-death experience that continues to mystify experts around the globe. Mark had read about Jim M. and Joe M and attempted to injure his own younger brother by smashing himself in the head with a hammer. He inadvertently crushed his own skull and was clinically dead for three days before regaining consciousness at his own wake. He was very grateful for the large number of people who showed up to pay their respects, and thanked them all profusely. Mark's brother, incidentally, felt nothing and sustained no injury at all. Apparently, it does not work between all brothers.

In multiple interviews, Mark has described the feeling of floating weightless and of seeing a bright white light. The light should have been blinding, but it wasn't. It emitted warmth, but did not burn. He felt compelled to move towards the light and he held his arms outstretched toward the light without fear. He was filled completely with love and joy while the gentle sounds of harps played somewhere off in the distance when, without any warning, the light went out and he was left in complete darkness.

He heard a voice say, "Hey Peter, the damn light went out again!! I thought you said you fixed the ******* thing!! Send this meat-head back to Earth. We'll have to get this thing fixed and send for him later."

Suddenly, Mark felt a pulling sensation. He wanted the light to come back on, because back on Earth he was in a loveless marriage and was in debt up to his eyeballs. Nevertheless, he was pulled back to his basement workshop where he was forced to spend the next twelve months recovering from his self-inflicted traumatic head injury.

According to Mark, he no longer has any fear of death. According to his wife, he no longer has unsupervised access to heavy, blunt objects.

And what of Elizabeth V. who was 7 years old when she first exhibited the ability to speak a language that she had never been taught and had never had any exposure to?

Her parents were dismayed and sought the opinions of experts and talk show hosts around the country. She spoke this foreign language with an astonishing fluency as if she'd been speaking it all of her life. Experts theorized that the young girl must have carried the knowledge of this enigmatic language over from a past life. Amazingly, no one was ever able match the guttural noises that she made with any known languages.

Scores of linguists studied the young girl searching for patterns or repetitive noises, but to no avail. One expert categorized her speech as "a severe Boston accent," but he was written off as a crackpot and drummed out of the industry.

Oddly enough, despite her comfort level with this mysterious tongue so complicated that the world's greatest experts were never able to decipher it, Elizabeth never was

● ● ●

able to grasp even the most rudimentary elements of the English language.

Perhaps the strangest of all was the story of Nick M. who claims to have undergone more than a hundred out-of-body experiences over the last three years.

His spirit would leave without warning and travel to distant lands, such as Las Vegas and Atlantic City, while poor Nick was left motionless in his home with no corroborating witnesses.

Nick's mischievous spirit ran up tens of thousands of dollars worth of credit card debt and racked up millions of frequent flyer miles. His spirit even committed bigamy by marrying some floozy down in Mexico City. Luckily for Nick, his wife understood that he had no control whatsoever over his spirit. She has stood by his side through thick and thin, but she is absolutely furious with his astral self.

Nick's spirit has apparently amassed a significant criminal record as well. It has been arrested on multiple occasions for disorderly conduct and public drunkenness. His spirit is often kept in a holding cell until it, "sleeps it off." Then it finally returns to Nick's body which has to endure a killer hangover.

Nick holds out the hope that his spirit will eventually settle down and enjoy the simple life of going to work five days a week and then visiting his in-laws on the weekends.

Yes, the world of the unknown is all around us. Perhaps your very neighbors have capabilities beyond the scope of modern knowledge. Perhaps they can read your mind, or can see right through your clothes, or something like that. If so, try to find some way to exploit their freakish nature for monetary compensation or, when that is not possible, feel free to persecute them for being different.

The Hermit and the Chickens From Hell

Editor's note: In preparation for a Halloween edition of the Town Crier, Steve Bjork was sent out on assignment to research the origins of a Wilmington legend surrounding a hermit that supposedly lived out in the woods somewhere between Ballardvale Street and Andover Street a hundred years ago. Mr. Bjork has uncharacteristically missed his deadline (and thus will not be paid) and has gone missing. We are not particularly worried, since Mr. Bjork has never been entirely stable, but we do have to fill this space. With nothing better on hand, we have no choice but to publish his most recent correspondence to this newspaper.

October 21

Shawn,

I have located the crumbling stone foundation of the Hermit's cabin deep in the woods and have set up camp here. I never realized how deep the woods could actually be in Wilmington.

I spent the first day searching for artifacts and evidence of the hermit's existence, with some success. In addition to the foundation are the remains of several animal pens and a number of, what appear to be, gravestones scattered about. Each of them is marked by the words "Chicken Feed." I'm not yet sure what to make of these.

The first night was unsettling to say the least. No lights or sounds could be seen in any direction and the only sounds to be heard were those of wild animals and, of course, my own whimpering.

I eventually fell into a fitful sleep and dreamed of the hermit. In my dream, he stood looming menacingly over me dressed in shabby brown clothes hanging loosely off him and secured around the waist by a tattered rope. He was very tall, though it was difficult to ascertain his exact height because he was wearing roller skates.

His face was sharp and angular with a hook of a nose. The whites of his eyes were mustard yellow and bloodshot. His hair was as black as the night with a mullet haircut. I offered him a breath mint, but he just brushed it away and proceeded to whisper horrible, awful things regarding unspeakable acts of violence and depravity into my ear. I resisted and tried several times to change the subject of conversation to various episodes of Seinfeld, but to no avail.

I awoke just after dawn without being sure how the dream ended, but with an unshakable feeling of dread and loneliness. I felt hundreds of miles from civilization. If it wasn't for the Post Office mailbox 50 yards away from my tent, all would be lost.

I was horrified to find the very breath mint from my dream outside my tent in a funky little pile of rocks that wasn't there when I went to sleep the night before. What the hell kind of ghost makes a pile of rocks? Has he nothing better to do with his time?

My nerves are shot, but I will continue researching this article for you, because...well, let's face it; ten bucks is ten bucks. I will keep you posted on my progress.

Regards,

Steve

Shawn,

Strange things are happening up here in the Town Forest. The hermit has appeared in each and every one of my dreams and has begun appearing during waking hours as well. His breath is even more offensive during daytime hours. I am beginning to fear for my very sanity.

Last night he tormented me with gruesome images of brutality, the likes of which I dare not record on paper. I fell to my knees; I clawed at the Earth and screamed for help. Afterwards, we played cribbage. I let him win, naturally.

Now, even in these brief moments of his absence, disturbing thoughts of savagery enter my head and must be pushed away.

I received your note regarding the paper's need to lower our agreed upon fee for this article. Yes, I do understand that the economy is difficult on corporations; especially as you explained that you had treated the office staff to lunch every day last week. Yes, I will continue for the newly negotiated fee, but I am really beginning to wonder if all of this is worth six bucks.

I will report my updated findings again in a day or two.

Regards,

Steve

October 25

Shawn,

Last night the hermit magically transported me back in time one hundred years and I saw how he lived.

I walked around his cabin and saw the animal pens. One had 40 or 50 chickens and was attached to a crudely fashioned hen house. The other was empty and left open. Seven large dogs followed me wherever I went, playfully darting back and forth and jumping up on me from time to time.

I began to have thoughts and memories that, while not completely alien, were not my own.

I wandered away from the cabin and came across a small pond. I knelt down to take a drink and saw that the reflection staring back at me from the water was that of the hermit. I shrieked and fell backwards, horrified at the sight. I would never have a mullet.

I tried desperately to run from that place, but alas, I was wearing roller skates, which made it extremely difficult.

I ran for, what seemed like miles, until I finally reached the site of his cabin. I was myself again and it was present day. Dawn came quickly then, but I remained a bit freaked out for the whole morning. That definitely weirded me out, man.

I think I would like to go home now. Do you think it would be okay to scratch the hermit piece? I am ok with forfeiting the six bucks. After all, it would only go so far after taxes anyway. Please advise at your earliest possible convenience.

Best Regards,
Steve

October 27

Shawn,

I have uncovered the truth about the hermit. Legend has it that his dogs turned on and devoured him, but that is not the case.

It was the chickens, Shawn, the chickens!

Oh, those horrible, vicious chickens. I was transported back in time once again tonight and I saw it happen right in front of my eyes. I stood frozen with fear as they tore him apart piece by piece without warning. They are truly messy eaters bereft of any table manners, whatsoever.

They were still hungry, and they looked at me with their beady chicken-eyes. They began to approach me, ready to strike at any moment.   The blessed dogs leapt to my defense, but ended up receiving the same fate as the poor hermit. These chickens are not of this world, I tell you. They are the spawn of the devil.   They are indeed Hell-Chickens walking the Earth looking for victims.

The dogs had satisfied their appetite for the moment, I guess, as they wandered off aimlessly.   Time shifted once again and brought me back to present day, but I cannot be lulled into a false sense of security. I have somehow become their portal through time and they are coming soon to claim me! Of that I have no doubt.

I am hiding under a layer of leaves here in the darkened forest with only a flashlight to write by. It will be several hours before the sun rises and I have little hope for my own survival. The chickens will be back.

Please, if you don't hear from me again, send the six bucks to my wife.

Oh my God, I hear clucking sounds. The clucking sounds are getting closer and closer;

louder and louder. They are almost right on top of me.

My terror is unmatched in the history of mankind and it kind of makes you wonder why someone in a situation like this would continue to write a stupid letter to his uncaring editor. Well, it's not because I couldn't think of a way to end this pitiful attempt at a ghost story, I can tell you that for sure.

Best Regards,

Steve

UFO's and Elvis

I recently wrote a column citing paranormal experiences and subsequently received a barrage of emails (two, actually) thanking me for uncovering that information and asking me to research recent UFO activity.

I liked the idea and set about to uncover the truth for once and for all. I interviewed hundreds of experts in the field (well, two, actually) and read volumes on the subject (well, two pamphlets, actually).

Recent studies in the field of UFO sightings and alien encounters have uncovered rather disturbing evidence. According to at least one UFO expert, extraterrestrials have successfully infiltrated our society posing as Elvis Presley impersonators.

Professor Thomas Anuria has been studying unexplained phenomenon for over six months and has published several papers on the subject. He is considered to be one of the top men in the field of UFO sightings and alien encounters and works fulltime as a greeter for Wal-Mart.

His theory asserts that the aliens come from a planet where no one has a personality of their own (conversations are only about the weather) so they have all decided to come to Earth and become Elvis. Anuria has termed these creatures "eliens" and assures us that these creatures live very normal unassuming lives; all things considered. The most successful eliens are working as Elvis impersonators in Vegas. Anuria supports his impersonator theory convincingly by pointing out, "Haven't you ever wondered about those guys?"

Eliens who are not able to support themselves as impersonators often hang around in K-Marts during the day, hoping to run into a photographer from the National Enquirer, and then they run to the karaoke bars at night.

Eliens, according to Anuria, are extremely territorial. Once a karaoke bar is claimed by an elien, no other elien is permitted entrance. Only an elien prepared to challenge the incumbent for rights to the bar will dare enter. A challenge can sometimes end in death for the loser, although it will generally end when one of the two begins crying.

Their territorialism, and potent body odor, explains why eliens do not associate with each other. It also explains why they still live with their mothers well into their late 40's.

Professor Anuria suggests a specific course of action when dealing with eliens, and he stresses that eliens are not evil or dangerous in any way.

"They are very simple-minded creatures who never have anything interesting to say. Almost childlike in their social graces," states Anuria. "They are probably more scared of you than you are of them."

The first, and best, option in dealing with these extremely boring life-forms is avoidance. Try to avoid them at all costs. They have been known to bore a human being to tears in less than fifteen seconds.

When avoidance is not an option, suggest that the elien sing his version of "Hound-dog." He will become enthralled in his own performance and your escape will go unnoticed.

One of the biggest mistakes one can make when dealing with an elien is to compliment him on the flashy white cape with the sequins and the colossal collar that they all have. The elien will immediately take it off, insist on your accepting it as his gift to you, and force you to wear it as he stands beside you smiling proudly.

Professor Anuria has many supporters in the field of unexplained phenomenon and in various laundromats around the country, but he is not without his share of critics. One of the most vocal of his critics is Dr. Michael Tragus.

Dr. Tragus considers himself to be a foremost authority in the field of alien research because he claims to have seen a UFO once and also because he has seen the movie E.T. one hundred and thirty-four times.

Tragus scoffs at Anuria's findings and points to drastically declining numbers of UFO sightings and abductions being reported in recent years.

Tragus says that aliens are not living among us as Elvis impersonators, but are simply big fans of the "King," and that they just don't visit Earth very much since his demise.

Tragus does agree with Anuria on one key point: aliens are extremely boring creatures. He has conducted countless interviews with people claiming to have been abducted by aliens and according to his subjects the aliens did not look anything like Elvis, and in fact, they looked startlingly like Ed Asner and refused to discuss anything except "Viva Las Vegas."

One abduction victim testified, under hypnosis (drunkenness, actually), that the aliens who abducted him boasted of attending more than two hundred Elvis concerts. They had an extensive collection of Elvis memorabilia and insisted on showing it to their human "guest."

The victim further stated, under hypnosis (still drunk), that the aliens performed no scientific experiments on him, but did fasten a crown on his head which would emit a mild electric shock if he referred to Elvis as anything but "The King." To this day, he still involuntarily wets his pants whenever he hears the name Elvis. Luckily he is from Maine, and his particular affliction goes unnoticed up there.

After several hours the aliens began to taunt him for his, "disgraceful" lack of knowledge of Elvis trivia. They snapped, however, when he could not even answer the question of Elvis's middle name. The leader smacked him on the head with a wooden cane, the head of which had been carved to resemble the "young" Elvis.

"Aaron, you idiot," they screamed over and over again, "Aaron!"

That man's head still has a small indent with the likeness of Elvis just over the right temple.

The aliens then tried to convince him that he had spent the previous few hours waiting for traffic signals to change. Then they dropped him into a cranberry bog. He claims to have distinctly heard them giggling uncontrollably as they zoomed off and into the sky.

Whether you believe Anuria or Tragus, one thing is certain: in one way or another, Elvis, the undisputed King of rock and roll, and extraterrestrials are hopelessly intertwined. So learn Elvis trivia well, and be careful at the karaoke bars.

To Spank, or Not To Spank

Do you remember spankings?

The disciplining of children has changed dramatically in the last 20 years or so. When many of us were kids spankings were a fact of life. Don't get me wrong here; I'm not talking about a psycho-mom-on-the-security-camera-of-the-mall-parking-lot type of spanking. I'm talking about mom and dad curtailing undesirable activities with prudence.

Back then mothers had their own personal arsenals. The lady down the street, for instance, used to threaten her kids with a hair brush. One of my friends used to get hit with his very own toys. The rest of us in the neighborhood used to giggle whenever she picked up the paddle-ball game. The little rubber ball would be bouncing all over the place as she whaled on his behind. That kid always had a very specific Christmas list: nothing but stuffed animals.

I even had a buddy whose mother would beat him with his own belt. How embarrassing is that? He'd be throwing rocks at cars or something and she'd walk up behind him, rip his little nylon belt right off his pants and give him a good couple of whacks with it. She used to scare me to death, but as an adult I can appreciate the beauty of that technique. Anytime he tried to run away his pants would fall down to his ankles and completely immobilize him, leaving him defenseless. I really felt bad for him and even bought him a pair of suspenders for his birthday one time.

My mother's weapon of choice was the wooden cooking spoon. I never realized that it could be used as a culinary tool until I was 21 years old.

She was truly lethal with that thing. According to family lore, my mother spent more than 16 years in Japan studying martial arts and weaponry, eventually becoming the deadliest woman in the world with a wooden spoon. I used to have dreams of her battling huge armies of samurais and ninja with nothing but two wooden spoons.

The funny thing is that I don't remember her ever actually using the spoon on us. She rarely even had to show us the spoon. My sister and I knew where it was kept and we didn't want that thing to be let loose on our little world for any reason. We could be doing something stupid three rooms away, or even on another floor of the house, and all my mother had to do was open up that drawer and start rustling around in it. My sister and I would immediately jump out the window and run twenty miles.

Dads don't need any weapons. All my dad had to do was grab me by the arm and pull me to him. All forward motion instantly ceased and I would find myself gazing in horror at my arm, completely swallowed up by his monstrous hairy mitt. I knew right then and there that I would do whatever needed to be done to avoid getting a spanking from that.

The grab was always accompanied by the unnecessary phrase, "Get over here."

Right. As if I had any other option.

Situations were handled so very differently back then. There is a heck of a lot more discussion today than there ever was when I was a kid.

"Now Billy, what did I tell you about shoving Kix cereal up your brother's nose?"

"You told me not to."

"That's right. So, why are you doing it right now?"

"I don't know."

"Well stop it."

"..."

"I said stop it right now, little mister. How are we going to get all of those Kix out of his nose?"

"..."

"I think someone is going to get a timeout. Oh, no you don't! Don't you even think about squeezing his nose with all of those Kix up there. They would break and give your brother boo-boos in his nose. Do you hear me talking to you?! Take your hand off of his nose...that's it buster! You are getting a time out! Where are you going? Get over here! Stop writing on that wall!"

Meanwhile the little brother is crying and it will easily take six months for his nostrils to fully recover from the Kix-shrapnel.

Can you imagine that same scenario thirty years ago?

SMACK!!

"Whaaaa!"

"Didn't I tell you never to shove Kix cereal up your brother's nose?! Don't do it again."

"Ok, Mom. I won't do it again."

Some people will tell you that the only thing you teach a child by hitting them is violence. Violence begets violence, blah, blah, blah.

Perhaps, but spanking always taught me the wonders of avoiding violence.

It all comes down to basic logic. Your mother told you a hundred thousand times not to touch the stove, because it is hot, but you touched it anyway didn't you? Yes, you did. She explained all about the boo-boos and the ouches and everything, but you didn't listen. You touched it and your own experience translated into logic and the logic said, "Ouch! Pain hurts. So that's what those two morons were talking about. I don't want to touch that stove again."

Back then it was a simple matter of cause and effect. For instance, if I set the couch on fire – which I am still not willing to admit to, by the way – and I got a spanking as a result, then I don't set the couch, or any other piece of furniture, on fire again.

Cause and effect can be a powerful teacher.

I learned the hard way that bees don't like it when you chuck a mess of your mom's garden tomatoes at their nest. In fact, they hate it. I didn't know any better; I was having a wonderful time. Then the bees began yelling obscenities at me and showed me their own particular version of "time out." Now, I know not to throw anybody's tomatoes at any bees' nests.

Turns out my mom was none too happy with my pilfering her tomatoes either. They were all green so I figured they weren't any good. What did I know? I was only 24 at the time.

Memories of Creature Double Feature

I miss the Channel 56 Creature Double Feature. If you grew up in New England during the late 70's and early 80's, before cable TV came on the scene, Channel 56 was a trusted and reliable friend. There were no remote controls back then and the only way for my father to channel surf through the 4 to 6 working channels was to set up a folding-chair next to the television and then duct tape me into it.

But back then, who needed to surf? Channel 56 provided everything we needed.

After school you could pull the on/off switch of the huge 26-inch color console television and then wait about 10 hours for the set to warm up enough to show a picture. Invariably you would have to adjust the tuner knob and antennae in order to get a picture. My house happened to be very high tech. The antenna on the roof was connected to a little box on top of the set. Twisting the knob on the box supposedly turned the antenna, which if it moved at all, did so at the speed of about one revolution per week. I still have my doubts that it did anything at all.

Banana Splits came on right after school and was followed by the staples of our generation: Gilligan's Island, The Brady Bunch, The Flintstones, Family Affair, and various other shows that were rotated in and out.

Channel 38 tried to compete, but catered to a slightly more mature audience with Barney Miller, M.A.S.H., The Rookies, and Adam 12.

The ultimate Channel 56 viewing time, as anyone in my generation will agree, was Saturday afternoons between 1:00 p.m. and 4:00 p.m. During those hours the street hockey nets were abandoned and no forts were being built. The streets were clear of children and the ice cream man made not a single nickel on Saturday afternoons.

My mother contends that the entire population of Wilmington, Massachusetts, those between the ages of 7 and 12 at any rate, was in my living room during those magic hours.

We'd all lie down on the mustard yellow shag carpeting (don't judge; it was the 1970's, remember) and just get ready to be scared out of our minds. We couldn't wait for the *VOICE* and theme music of the Creature Double Feature to come on. Looking back on it, those two aspects were often the scariest part of the whole afternoon. The music was an edited version of "Toccata" by Emerson, Lake, and Palmer; an eerie, gothic sort of music with an overwhelming sense of inescapable doom. To this day it still puts "the fear" into me.

The *VOICE* never appeared on camera, so his appearance was left up to our vivid imaginations.

His name was Cecil and with such a voice he had to be misshapen and grotesque. Perhaps he was created in a lab like Frankenstein, we used to wonder. Maybe he looked more like the hunchback. Every week we described him to each other and every one of us had our own individualized image of his monstrous deformities, but we all agreed on two things: he scared the life out of us and we never wanted to meet him.

Then all of a sudden the clock would strike one o'clock and it would happen.

"Helloooo…and welcome to the CREATURE DOUBLE FEATURE."

THAT'S THE GUY!!!

● ● ●

Phoooosh! 1,300 little kids would duck behind my sofa at the speed of light leaving a few random Legos to hang momentarily in the air before falling to the floor.

Not one of us had the courage to peek out as he announced the name of the two monster movies to be aired that day. In fact, I think most of us clenched our eyes shut tight until he stopped speaking. Only with the onset of ominous theme music from some 1950's "B" science fiction, or straight up monster movie, would we dare to come out from the safety-shield of a 1970's re-upholstered sofa.

Those 1950's movies used to scare us to pieces. I remember *The Brain That Wouldn't Die* as particularly terrifying. In that movie a really bad actor, who also happens to be a scientist and surgeon, crashes his car for no apparent reason at all. His fiancé happens to be decapitated during the accident, which is convenient to the plot. Fortunately, the tragic accident takes place within walking distance of his secluded laboratory. He gathers up her skull-piece and carries it back to the lab.

He sticks her head in a turkey-roasting pan filled with life-giving serums and props her upright with a set of tinker-toys. Despite the beheading, she has not a scratch on her face, nor is her make-up smudged in the least.

The only problem mucking up the works is that she does not want to be just a head.

The good doctor has a plan. He will visit every sleazy strip club in creation to find a smokin' hot body for his fiancé's needy head. She is not down with that plan, however, and would rather be left alone to die. It is tough to unplug your own life support system, however, when you have no hands, arms, or torso.

Naturally, the doctor has a faithful assistant. The assistant happens to have a severely mangled hand. To round out the movie's cast, there is a hideous monster in the closet (the monster is not gay; he is literally kept in a closet).

To make a long story short, the head establishes some sort of psychic connection with the monster, who escapes and tears off the assistant's bad arm (it wasn't doing him much good anyway) and eventually sets a fire, which consumes the doctor, the head, and the monster.

Boy, that was a great one. Whenever they played that movie I wouldn't be able to sleep for weeks.

It Conquered the World was another one that kept me up at night. It starred Peter Graves, who would later use nearly identical dialogue and demeanor for comic effect in the "Airplane!" movies.

"It" refers to a creature from Venus who hitches a ride to Earth on a satellite and then hides in a cave for the majority of the movie. Apparently, Venusians are not much into cardio.

The alien gestates several lobster-bat-like creatures, to go implant mind control devices into all the influential people in town. It is explained that It can only create five of these mind-control creatures at a time, so it must be quite choosey about the targets. That being said, It targets the commander of the neighboring Air force base, the Barney Fife town sheriff, and a couple of housewives.

Infected people generally walk around without emotion and conspire to infect Peter Graves, who has so far eluded the flying lobster sent for him.

Graves' best friend, of course, has been aiding the Venusian the whole time and doesn't see the error of his ways until his own wife marches into the cave to confront the alien. She is not very bright and the alien kills her immediately.

The highlight of the film comes near the end when we finally get to see the monster. The movie should have ended just prior to the sighting, quite frankly. It has no visible legs and is best described as a giant cucumber with vampire fans and crab arms.

"It" never really comes anywhere near conquering the world. It wasn't even able to conquer a hillbilly town. In fact, a small number of rather dimwitted soldiers manage to stave it off while Grave's friend kills it with his - convenient - new invention.

We always had the most fun, however when some giant monster would beat the stuffing out of Tokyo.

Godzilla truly was top of the heap for us. He was a bad guy in his first movie, but in all the sequels he was the good guy (kind of like Arnold Schwarzenegger in the Terminator series) pounding the snot out of some other monster.

My living room was never more crowded than when they played Godzilla vs. The Smog Monster. Great action in that one and tremendous special effects for a couple of adults wandering around in rubber monster suits with poorly designed eye-holes.

The Smog Monster didn't have much of a career in movies after that, but did end up with a major role in the television series "Sigmund & the Sea Monsters." According to sources, he was one of Sigmund's evil brothers.

Gamera was a cool monster. He was a giant turtle who could fly and spit fire, but presently lives in the "where is he now" file. Most recent reports say he ended up selling used auto parts in Nevada.

The War of the Gargantuas was also one of the most popular films in the neighborhood. It involved two giant hairy monsters. They were brothers, but were not the same color, so they probably had different fathers.

The brown Gargantua was good and the Green one was bad. In other words, the brown one liked people and the green one liked people with ketchup. Or, to put it yet another way, the brown one liked to cook breakfast for people and the green one liked to cook people for breakfast.

The green one always spit out the clothes of his victims. Apparently textiles suffer from a lack of flavor. The brown one would get really mad whenever he would see chewed up clothes lying on the ground, not only because he liked people, but also because he was a conservationist who hated pollution.

All of the Rubber Suit Movies ended with a major battle and then the fine people of Japan would quickly and optimistically rebuild Tokyo.

Tokyo has apparently remained intact since Creature Double Feature went off the air way back when, but the neighborhood kids have never quite accepted its cancellation. They are now in their mid-forties and still show up at my parents' house on Saturdays.

For my sake, the sake of the neighborhood kids, and most of all for my mother's sake, I hope someone finds a way to get Creature Double Feature back on the air. Just don't wake up Cecil. I'm sure he is better left undisturbed.

The One Year Anniversary

Editor's Note: December 4th marks the one-year anniversary of the first appearance of the Standing Eight Count in this newspaper. It has appeared more than thirty times since then and we are thus far yet to rid ourselves of it.

On the basis of the extensive popularity of the Standing Eight Count, baffling though it is, the Arts & Entertainment television network has chosen Steve Bjork as the subject of an upcoming episode in their Biography series. We have invited Mr. Edwin Naloxone, Producer and Director of the proposed production, to step in this week as a guest columnist.

I remember, quite vividly, my first conversation with Steve Bjork.

I must admit to feeling an immediate distrust of him, but that was soon replaced by a genuine dislike.

I had been reading his Standing Eight Count since it first began running in the Los Angeles Daily Tribune sometime in June of this year, as had most everyone else in the office.

Mr. Bjork's name came up during a departmental pitch meeting for upcoming programming as a possible subject for a Biography profile. The task fell on me to contact him and to conduct the preliminary research for the program.

One should note that it is unheard of in the newspaper business for a columnist to achieve national syndication in such a short span of time. Indeed, despite the amateurish prose and the frequently violent undertones of his work, Mr. Bjork's column has been picked up by more than 500 newspapers nationwide and has been described by some as a true zeitgeist for the current era. The column has, in fact, recently been nominated for a Pulitzer Prize for social and political commentary. Furthermore, a number of insiders feel that it has more than a fair shot of winning, despite the lingering rumors that it was Mr. Bjork himself who made the initial nomination.

Quite an accomplishment for a writer possessing such a wide-ranging lack of talent and wardrobe.

It was two o'clock in the afternoon, Los Angeles time, when I first dialed his number. I distractedly began to scan some of his previous columns and nearly forgot that his phone had been ringing on the other end for more than five minutes. I was just about to hang up when the receiver on the other end of the line was clumsily picked up and apparently hurled to the floor. A rash of obscenities was erupting from some distance away and, as the receiver was finally picked up off the floor, I was greeted not by the customary and pleasant greeting of "hello," but by the demand, "Who is this?"

It was eleven a.m. Boston time on a Wednesday and I had very obviously woken him.

I stuttered for just a moment in explaining the reason for my intrusive phone call and he began to calm down a bit.

I described my vision for the special. Certain segments could be done in black and white to highlight the darker side of some of his humor and we could experiment with camera angles and lighting to achieve the proper perspective. "How much would something like this pay?" he inquired repeatedly.

Mr. Bjork has had quite a busy year since he began writing his column.

He traveled to North Korea in February and was granted a private audience with that nation's sick and twisted leader, Kim Jong Il. The two spent more than 48 hours together, during which time Mr. Bjork's personal

• • •

interpreter was reportedly executed for not being able to speak Korean.

I must say, we managed to get some great footage of Kim Jong Il recalling the time he spent with Mr. Bjork, whom he describes as the single greatest cause for international tension today. Jong also claims to have lent Mr. Bjork twenty dollars, which has yet to be repaid.

In late March, Mr. Bjork mounted a write-in campaign for a seat on Wilmington's Board of Selectmen garnering a surprising .000000000 percent of the town vote. Political analysts uniformly agree that his promises to bring martial law and organized crime to Wilmington, if elected, probably contributed somewhat to his embarrassing loss.

Mr. Bjork was reportedly engaged in a physical altercation with Saddam Hussein in mid-April following the ousted dictator's disappearance from Iraq and subsequent "pop-in" visit to Mr. Bjork's home. Unfortunately, American authorities were not alerted in time to execute a successful apprehension.

Hussein was not available for an on-camera interview, but sent word via the Aljirah news network that he met Mr. Bjork on a particularly bad day and could ordinarily kick his butt any day of the week and, according to Hussein, twice on Sundays.

Pepe, Bjork's childhood friend, was not a particularly good subject for our filming as he kept repeating, "No comprende," after every question. Furthermore, he subjected each member of the A&E crew to unnecessary Heimlich Maneuvers making it increasing difficult to keep him on camera.

Shawn Sullivan is Mr. Bjork's editor at the Town Crier and consented to be interviewed on camera. Sullivan, who is considered one of the most supportive and encouraging editors in the newspaper industry, describes Mr. Bjork as a "no talent hack, without an ounce of creativity."

"He generally hands in a bunch of non-sensible scribbling, written in crayon," Sullivan states on camera. "I generally toss it into the trash and write the column myself. I never expected it to take off like this. We're not filming yet, are we?"

Stuart Neilson is the Managing Editor of the Town Crier and claims never to have met Mr. Bjork in person and is not entirely convinced that he exists. When asked to comment on the Standing Eight, he describes it as, "generally, very long."

The Town Crier has two receptionists, Ann and Mary; neither of whom consented to an interview. When asked, Ann simply opened her jacket revealing a 9mm automatic pistol. Mary pretended not to hear the question and said, "Good morning, Town Crier," even though it was late in the afternoon.

Extensive research of Mr. Bjork's childhood was conducted by me and my staff. Several of his former teachers and guidance counselors were contacted. Most refused to participate in the project in any way, but a few agreed to appear provided we guaranteed to keep their faces off camera and to alter their voices. One high school report card unearthed contained comments from a guidance counselor indicating that the young Mr. Bjork would never amount to anything.

"See, I told you," the guidance counselor stated for the camera.

We were a little bit taken aback when Mr. Bjork showed up for his on-camera interview wearing a silk smoking jacket and ascot. He insisted on speaking with an English accent and smoking a pipe throughout the entire production. He compared himself, and favorably so, to such "American writers" as F. Scott Fitzgerald, Ernest Hemingway, and Anton Chekhov (Chekhov, incidentally, was not American at all, but was a 19th century Russian author).

● ● ●

We ended up getting nothing of value out of his interview and, with the exception of the Kim Jong II footage, we had nothing to work with.

A&E executives stepped in and put a halt to the project, and that stoppage turned out to be well timed. According to sources, The Standing Eight Count has recently been dropped from 499 different newspapers.

Let it Snow

Let it snow, let it snow, let it snow.
I would love to meet the guy who wrote those lyrics and punch him right in the face.

We haven't even hit the official first day of winter and I'm sick and tired of the sight of snow; specifically, when it sits on my driveway and on my vehicles. I'd rather be in a 6-foot by 8-foot hole in the ground with a semi-obstructed view of the Baghdad royal palaces than in this New England winter right now.

No matter how hot it got, I never complained over the past summer. Not even once. Last winter was too brutal for me to forget. People around me complained about the heat and humidity and I always said the same thing: Those are two things that I will never have to shovel off of my driveway.

"Let's widen the driveway," I told my wife last July in the midst of a brief bout with amnesia. She agreed.

That was a decision that could only have been made in the height of summer. No one ever finished shoveling 14 inches of snow off their driveway and thought, "Boy, I wish this thing was bigger."

I do have a snow-blower, which is extremely efficient in removing the snow from my driveway by throwing it up high into the air for the wind to deposit directly onto my exposed face and down the back of my neck.

The snow-blower hasn't done me a whole lot of good so far this year. The first storm left something like 22 inches of heavy snow and I learned a brand new word: Shear Pin. I may be spelling it incorrectly, but most men won't recognize it anyway unless I place it into the proper context. Most snow-blower owners know it only as the f*****g Shear Pin; as in, "I broke another f*****g Shear Pin and I've only got a quarter of the f*****g driveway done."

It can occasionally be used to your advantage, because when that pin snaps you are out of commission until you can get a replacement. I've known a couple of guys who will snap that pin on purpose just so they can call a plow and watch the game.

This latest storm was far worse than the first. The snow was wet and slushy, which offers the ideal conditions for clogging up the chute on your trusty snow-blower. It was also a pleasant way for me to discover that my boots are no longer water proof.

Very few things in life are more maddening than watching helplessly as the chute, which was throwing very nicely for about a foot and a half, suddenly clogs up. It is reminiscent of the climactic scene from any action movie. You see it happening in front of you, but you're powerless to stop it.

You hear the engine begin to struggle and the snow coming out of the chute thickens up and isn't so much thrown as vomited. It all seems to be taking place in slow motion. You can see it all unfolding before you, the snow being thrown from the chute forms visible ripples in the air and each clump appears as clearly as the speeding bullet effect from those Matrix movies. Tragically, your reaction time is also stuck in slow motion and you aren't able to respond in time to stop the inevitable progression.

You pull back on the handles as quickly as possible, hoping beyond hope that the machine will free itself up. Throughout the entire process you are screaming the action-hero mantra of, "Noooooooooooo!"

You're too late. It's clogged again.

After clearing the chute for the millionth time with a broom handle, and clearing a total of 10 feet worth of driveway over the course of the last three hours, strange thoughts begin to enter your head. You see that big DANGER decal on the chute with the dramatic picture of a stick figure getting his hand cut off and you think, "I'll bet that stick figure doesn't have to clean his driveway anymore."

I was really excited when I first got my "Toro 824 XL Power Throw" a few years ago. Following the first good snowfall I cleared off my driveway, two of my neighbors' driveways, the patio in my backyard, a series of paths to different areas of my yard, the local plaza parking lot, and the southbound side of I-93 between Dascomb Road and Ballardvale Street.

The operator's manual was ready for me, because it specifically advises against using the snow-blower on your roof; otherwise I might have.

I'm not kidding. Item number 22 under the Safety While Operating section of the manual says, "Do not use snowthrower on a roof."

Good advice. Probably saved my life.

Alas, the thrill of it all seems to have left me, however. Such is the plight of the typical American.

When I had a shovel I dreamed of a snow-blower.

Now I have a snow-blower and I am dreaming of a truck with a plow.

Most likely, if I had a truck with a plow I would dream of a home in Florida.

The truth is I've got something better than any of those things. I have a son, and he is old enough to handle a shovel.

Soon he will dream of snow-blowers and plows.

Dieting and the Dieting Dieters Who Diet

Why do dieters assume that you have been waiting all day just to hear about every single morsel of food that has been thrown into their gullet for the past four days?

The conversation always starts the same way.

"Do you know what I've had to eat today?" the dieter asks.

"Yes, I do," I say, hoping beyond hope that this will provide some sort of a close to the topic. Alas, they seem not to hear.

"For breakfast, all I had was one egg white, a half a slice of dry wheat toast, and four ounces of orange juice."

"How 'bout them Patriots this year?" I ask.

"Then for lunch I had a half a can of dry tuna with one piece of iceberg lettuce."

"Can't wait for regular season to start up," I say, well aware of the futility of my statement.

"And yesterday, all day, all I had was a breath mint. And y'know what? I wasn't even hungry."

There is only one effective way to combat these conversations. Go ahead and tell them what you've had to eat that day - and don't be afraid to make stuff up.

"That's all you had for breakfast? Don't you know that breakfast is the most important meal of the day?" I begin. "This morning I had Belgian waffles with strawberry sauce and a ton of whipped cream, but I didn't finish them because I suddenly got the urge for a nice big stack of pancakes covered in butter and maple syrup. Y'ever get a sudden urge for a particular kind of food like that? Oh, yeah, and I had a half-pound of bacon!"

A subtle tick begins to develop in their left eyelid at this point.

"Then for lunch I started with a three-scoop hot fudge ice cream sundae. I figured what the hell; I can always start my diet tomorrow, right? You only live once after all. Then I had this incredible pasta dish with a heavy white cream sauce packed with seafood. I don't think I have ever tasted anything that good before."

Even if the recitation of your recent food choices doesn't adequately demonstrate the boring nature of the subject, it will generally knock them off their diet. Either way, problem solved; they won't be telling you what they are eating anytime soon.

I am convinced that Weight Watchers is a cult.

Their "Higher Power" is the Point System. Their members walk around all day assigning point values to various food products and insisting that you become aware of the corresponding value of whatever you happen to be putting in your mouth.

"What'ya got there?" they ask. "Chips? That's four points right there, buddy. I can cook a whole skinless chicken breast for only two and a half points. I can even add 10 hazelnuts to it adding only one more point. Plus, I can eat all the cabbage I want."

Oh, really? What if you were to eat a bullet? How many points in a bullet?

I also love people who have no idea *why* they are overweight.

"All I have to do is look at chocolate and I gain ten pounds," they say.

If you have ever made that statement, trust me; looking at chocolate is not your problem. It's not a problem for anyone on Earth. The problem is that when you think no one is looking at you, you shove chocolates down your throat like they are discarded Christmas trees and your mouth is wood chipper.

These are the same people that will dejectedly point at their skinny friend and claim that he/she can eat anything they want and not gain a single ounce.

True enough. The difference is that he/she doesn't seem to want to eat half as much as fatty does. Thin people just don't feel an overwhelming need to "get their money's worth" at the all-you-can-eat buffet.

Do you have two friends like that? Take them both out for drinks sometime. Order a basket of French fries and sit back and watch the show. Conversation continues unabated, but suddenly the basket is empty and fatty is using his index finger to wipe up the residual fry grease from the wax paper while ole' skin-and-bones has eaten a total of three fries.

Yep, it's true; he can eat all he wants and never gains an ounce.

I know of what I speak. I just so happen to be big-boned. Thank God I'm big-boned, because my big bones are carrying around a lot of extra pounds. I was born with a perfectly good birthday-suit, but now it is all stretched out. There is no secret as to why I have these excessive pounds - I eat too much and I don't exercise enough. Case closed.

Wow, what a revelation that was.

Being overweight, like it or not, is a choice – or more accurately, it is a series of small choices that we make every day. Yes, the pace of my metabolism seems to rival that of a two-week old corpse, but that is just an excuse.

I tried the Atkins diet for two weeks last year, but it just didn't seem right. Can you imagine telling someone during the 1980's that you were sitting down to a bacon and cheese omelet because you were on a diet?

An entire generation had been taught to count calories and fat content. Every food manufacturer in the world developed low-fat or fat-free products. One of the few things that they weren't able to remove the fat from was good old fashioned bacon and it was considered the evilest of all foods. Then all of a sudden, along comes this Atkins guy and turns the diet world upside down.

"Go ahead, silly; eat the bacon," Atkins said. "I don't know what they were thinking, telling you to stay away from the bacon like that. Sorry, man. How about pork rinds? Do you like those? Go ahead and eat as many pork rinds as you can stomach."

I was in love with this guy, Atkins. Sure I missed pasta, bread, potatoes, fruit, donuts, pizza, Chinese food, fried foods of any kind, soda, and especially beer, but hey, bacon is good.

I'm geared up for the newest diet fad. Very few people are aware of it yet, but it's creating quite a stir down south. On this diet, you are not allowed to eat anything unless it comes out of a fryolater. It's called the Kevorkian Diet.

Man Caves

Where is your Man Cave?

A Man Cave, for those unfamiliar with the term, is that area of a man's property devoted to his "cool" stuff and completely devoid of any female consultations. Every guy needs one, no matter how meager it may be.

Don't mistake the Man Cave with the Workshop. The Workshop is where you keep all your tools and where you pretend to do home improvement-related projects. Sure power-tools are fun, but there are no tools in a Man Cave – unless, of course, you consider a bottle opener a tool.

A picture-perfect Man Cave would consume an entire wing of an estate and would include a minimum of six hi-def televisions mounted side by side on a wall, a full-sized pool table, dartboard, extensive sports memorabilia, and a fully stocked bar complete with refrigerator and draft beer system. What the heck, we might as well include 24-hour waitress service in that dream scenario.

A typical Man Cave may include a wall-mounted deer's head, complete with party hat and scarf, along with other equally tacky decorations such as lighted beer signs, fraternity banners, lava lamps – basically anything your wife tried to pack away in the attic when you moved out of your bachelor pad. In fact, any item that your wife has ever pointed disgustedly at and said, "There is no way *that thing* is going anywhere near our house," is generally an ideal addition to your own personal Man Cave.

One of those hats that holds two beer cans and has a straw leading from both cans to the wearer's mouth, for example, is a tremendous addition to any Man Cave. Those hats are best displayed on the deer head or on a ventriloquist dummy.

A tasteful display of your vintage Star Wars action figures that you've had since you were a kid provides a nice touch to any Man Cave. The ultimate Man Cave nostalgia toy for display purposes, however, would be an authentic GI-Joe with the Kung-Fu Grip.

By the way, if you do not have room for a pool table, do not; and I cannot stress this enough, make the mistake of bringing in a bumper-pool table. I have seen this mistake several times when I was just a kid and I never forgot it.

Number one – a bumper-pool table will cost you the respect of all your buddies. What full grown man would be caught betting money on a serious game of bumper pool?

Number two – with the addition of bumper-pool, your room will have immediately been transformed from a Man Cave to a Playroom. Kids will invade the space and you will be left sitting dejectedly in some stupid beanbag chair (that your wife put in for the kids) watching the PowerPuff girls on your 60-inch screen.

You've got to have at least one big puffy leather reclining chair in your Man Cave.

Men don't care if reclining chairs are tacky; they are indescribably comfortable. In fact, if you run down to Building 19 you can probably find one with a built in cooler and vibrating-massage feature. While women may be opposed to recliners in general, they go absolutely ballistic watching someone plug an a/c adapter into a piece of furniture.

Recliners rule. Why do men love them? Because they are basically Craftmatic adjustable beds for the living room. You can sit up straight, put your feet up, or lie all the way back and "rest your eyes" while the game is on.

Not all men have an idyllic Man Cave of their very own, but they can, and will, make due with whatever happens to be available. I know guys that have very successfully set up impressive Man Caves, with all the necessary accoutrements, in their unfinished basements and garages. I've even heard tales of some poor souls resorting to a flimsy ramshackle aluminum shed out in the corner of their lot. We'll do what we have to.

I have one unfortunate buddy whose Man Cave is set up in the crawl space underneath his rear deck. Poor guy. I feel bad, so I go over once in a while. We get down on our bellies and shimmy underneath the lattice and then we lie in the dirt, drink beer, and talk about old times. It's really kind of sad.

Some guys are afraid to tell their wives about their Man Caves and they keep them hidden.

"Honey?" the wife calls up the attic's fold-out stairs. "You've been up there a long time; are you still putting in the new roof?"

"That's right Sweetie-pie and this will probably take quite a bit of my spare time for the foreseeable future. This is in much worse shape than I originally estimated," the frightened husband replies.

"I thought a new roof was put on from the outside."

"Uhh, this is a much more effective way for, uh, stabilization and structural reasons having to do with the, uh, wood-to-shingle ratio and plus I have to do less, uh, routing this way."

"Honey, why do I hear Cinemax coming out of the attic?"

There are many ways to detect a hidden Man Cave - an extension cord leading out to the tree-fort is a dead giveaway, especially if your kids are in college.

I will tell you right now that I am King of my castle (my wife gave me permission to say that) and the number one rule of my own personal Man Cave is: NO CANDLES.

Candles are a sure sign that a Man Cave has been compromised. If you find that a Man Cave belonging to one of your friends has been infected with even one candle, get out as quickly as possible. Don't look back and don't try to help your friend; cut all ties with him and save yourself before it is too late.

Once the infection begins it is just a matter of time before the windows are given "treatments" and family pictures begin to appear all over the walls. The next thing you know, you and your wife are sitting right there with he and his wife in the newly remodeled "Family Room." By that point you can kiss your own Man Cave goodbye; it's a goner.

"You know what, honey? This gives me some ideas for that room of yours," your own wife says.

All of a sudden the crawl space idea won't sound so bad.

Janet Jackson Lets Loose at the Big Game

Chances are you were sitting in front of the television on the first Sunday in February 2004. Chances are, also, that you were jumping up and down, high-five'ing and cheering in front of that television.

And that was just the halftime show.

Did you enjoy Superbowl XXXVIII-Double-D?

It was fantastic television, no doubt about it. After all, it's not often that you get a chance to see celebrity-boob on network television.

Plus, there was a football game on.

That's right, the Patriots won their second world championship in just three short years...and we got to see one of Janet Jackson's boobs (the right one, to be specific). What a night!

People were outraged by the display of Jackson's exposed Taa-Taa, which all but dominated the news of the following week. I myself am outraged. I mean, c'mon - as a matter of simple parity, equal viewing time should have been granted to the left one as well. Fair is fair.

For those who were offended, please remember; it could have been worse – it could have been Justin Timberlake's scrawny little chest that was exposed.

Just in case you had been living in a cave or spider-hole in the winter of 2004, Janet Jackson performed during the halftime show and proved once and for all that, despite persistent rumors, she is not Michael Jackson in drag.

During a musical number, Timberlake, an alleged singer, pulled off a piece of Jackson's bustier revealing one of her

Winnebagos, which was clad only in - and I'm not making this up; it is in the Associated Press release – "a sun-shaped nipple shield."

Personally, I am more offended by the media's blatant use of the term "nipple shield" than in the actual event.

Timberlake apologized after the game and blamed it on a "wardrobe malfunction." Yeah, apparently he didn't realize that fabric tore when pulled.

Jackson also issued an apology for her little game of peek-a-boob. In a statement released to the Associated Press the following Monday night she categorized it as a last minute decision.

"The decision to have a costume reveal at the end of my halftime show performance was made after final rehearsals. MTV was completely unaware of it. It was not my intention that it go as far as it did. I apologize to anyone offended," Jackson told the Associated Press while reportedly removing her pants.

Janet! You've just ruined the Superbowl! Where are you going now?!

"I'm going to Silicon Valley!"

Rumors have recently begun to circulate that Jackson and Timberlake considered kissing at the end of their portion of the halftime show. They reportedly scrapped the idea because the taboo of two women kissing on mainstream television had already been broken several months earlier by Britney Spears and Madonna on MTV.

Federal Communications Commission Chief, Michael Powell, announced a full scale investigation into the matter. He reportedly promised to leave no stone or brassiere unturned in his search for the truth and, although he was greatly offended, he would be forced to watch the video of the infamous "reveal" over and over again, sometimes in slow motion and sometimes in reverse, until he uncovers the bare truth.

I wish somebody would put me in charge. I could have completed that investigation before the halftime show was over.

I would point at the television and say, "I see a naked booby! Levy fines against CBS and all the affiliates carrying the broadcast!"

How much more investigating really needs to be done to solve this great mystery?

"Hi, am I speaking with the boss of CBS?"

"Yes, that's me."

"I am conducting a full scale investigation into the scandal known as Boob-gate."

"Okay."

"Did you know it was going to happen beforehand?"

"No."

"Are you sure?"

"Yup."

"Damn. I'm not sure where to go from here. I better watch the video again."

Maybe network executives knew about it or maybe they didn't; it doesn't much matter. If the FCC wants to prevent such an atrocity in the future, they need to spend less time "investigating" the matter and more time putting the screws to Jackson and Timberlake.

Those two half-wits got exactly what they wanted – a staggering amount of publicity; the kind that all the money in the world couldn't buy. You couldn't turn on a radio or a television on the following Monday or Tuesday without hearing about Jackson's boobs – and no one was referring to her brothers.

Any celebrity in the world will tell you that there is no such thing as bad publicity. Disagree? Rush Limbaugh's ratings increased dramatically, with various affiliates across the country registering increases of between 8 and 23 percent, upon his return to the airwaves after a five-week stay in a drug rehab program for an admitted addiction to painkillers.

If the FCC really wants to send a message they should have encouraged the network to sue her and Timberlake both into a state of absolute indigence. That and that alone, would convince Jackson, and others like her, to keep her melons safely on the produce shelves while on national television.

You don't see a whole lot of women on skid row sporting ornate nipple shields.

No Brakes!

In January 2004, a woman from Colorado was in a car that accelerated out of control and took her on a 75-mile ride at speeds of 100 mph.

According to the Associated Press, 20-year-old Angel Eck was traveling on I-70 when her 1997 Pontiac Sunbird began racing out of control and her brakes failed.

"Nothing she tried would slow the car down," according to the AP account.

The AP explains that the vehicle's brakes failed to work, and then goes on to explain some of the other techniques that Eck (rough last name, by the way) incorporated in her attempts to slow the vehicle. Apparently she flipped on her hazard lights and dodged traffic while trying to use her cell phone, but alas, she was out of her service area.

I'm not making that up.

The report goes on to say that after 45 minutes of frantic attempts; she was finally able to reach a friend on her cell phone.

Maybe it's just me, but I think it might be more prudent to dial 911 and keep hitting redial rather than trying to reach every like-minded dolt in your address book.

Police were finally able to slow her down by positioning a cruiser in front of her car and slowing down gradually. Six cruisers were involved and the entire highway was cleared.

I've read at least five or six accounts of this story and I haven't heard anyone ask if she ever tried to turn the ignition off. Sure the power-steering would be gone, but she was on a highway with no sharp turns. Or did she even attempt something as simple as shifting into neutral or low gear?

I'm no mechanic and I could be dead wrong, but how many things could have malfunctioned on her car at once? Was this a real life episode of the Rockford Files?

Okay, the accelerator is jammed AND my brakes are gone. That's dangerous and bad luck to boot, but what are the chances that the transmission is locked into drive?

Uh, oh, it is. I can't seem to shift into neutral, what a freaky coincidence!

That's okay, I can just switch off the ignition.

Nope, the ignition is locked too. This is not my day. It's a good thing I've got my nipple shields in place.

Comic Books

I was a comic book fanatic when I was a kid.

The best place to buy old comic books was at a weekly flea market held every Sunday in North Reading. Every week, my buddy Jim and I would ride our bikes to the flea market with wads of money earned from paper routes and lawn mowing.

Jim has been, and remains, one of my closest friends since we met in first grade. By the time we were making our weekly trek, Jim was known in town for two things.

Number one: he would take his Red Line BMX bike over any jump, no matter how intimidating or dangerous. Kids in the neighborhood were determined to see him back down; they spent hours devising and building intricate ramps for him to jump over picnic tables, streams, Interstate 93; anything to test his mettle. He never once backed down from a jump challenge.

Number two: by the age of 14 he had suffered more concussions than anyone else in the state, regardless of age.

For a time, during our early teens, Jim suffered concussions on nearly a weekly basis and was known by name to the entire staff at the Wilmington Health Center. In fact, his mother once got a call from the Health Center inquiring of Jim's well-being, since he'd not been in for treatment in nearly a month.

See, back then the idea of putting a bicycle helmet on a child never occurred to any of the adults. The only skull protection Jim had was a big, puffy, 70's haircut. It didn't help much.

I soon became known around town as "the kid who took Jim to the Health Center." As far as monikers go, it could have been worse.

In those days, bicycle riding was one of the purest forms of Darwinism. No helmets and an unforgiving cold metal bar running between the seat and the handlebars. I always thought that the metal bar was a conscious effort to encourage the process of natural selection - those reckless enough to come crashing down on that evil hunk of steel more than once were surely jeopardizing their ability to eventually procreate. My theory, however, was dashed several years ago – Jim has three kids and they all appear fairly normal.

At any rate, there was a booth at the flea market with thousands upon thousands of comics, and we spent every penny every week. We had our favorites of course - Spiderman, Daredevil, and the X-Men; but if it was printed by Marvel, we had to have it.

Marvel Comics had, and no doubt still has, thousands of superheroes and super-villains; all with their own unique super-powers. A vast majority of them gained those super-powers through some type of exposure to radiation. Bruce Banner, for instance was transformed into the Hulk after exposure to a bomb containing gamma radiation. Spiderman gained his abilities after being bitten by a radioactive spider. Daredevil was struck in the eyes by radioactive isotopes.

When you accept the premise that radioactivity could alter a person's DNA code and provide superhuman attributes, you must also accept the likelihood that there must be an equal number of people who received, in similar circumstances, completely ineffectual "super-powers."

For instance, what if you were bitten by a radioactive sloth? What a bummer that would be. Surely you would gain the attributes of a sloth, but that wouldn't make you a very valuable crime-fighter by any standards.

You'd be a pathetic individual blessed with super-human levels of laziness, indolence, and a "sloth-sense" enabling you to avoid work or exertion. You could adopt the identity of Slothman! The World's Slowest Moving Man.

You'd never get your own comic book.

If Slothman did have his own comic book it would pretty much consist of a bitter, overweight underachiever hanging upside down from a tree branch installed in his living room and eating leaves all day while complaining to his friends about his lot in life.

Then again, if he was unable to avoid being bitten by a sloth, radioactive or not, he probably wasn't going around breaking any land speed records in any case.

I was bitten by a squirrel once. He was on the edge of a four-foot stone wall and I was feeding him pieces of a cracker. He was getting progressively closer to taking it right out of my hand with each piece. Finally, he decided to go for broke and made a lunge for the cracker in my hand. Unfortunately for both of us, he missed the cracker. All of a sudden he was off balance and had to make a split second decision - clamp down on something quick or fall flat on his little squirrel face. The only thing available for clamping was my index finger, and he went for it.

Instinctively I pulled my hand back and started shaking it, which afforded him no alternative but to hang on like it was a carnival ride; otherwise he'd be thrown to the ground. I swung him and danced around like an epileptic gymnast doing a floor routine with a ribbon-thingy for a full minute and a half before he finally found an opening to let go.

I sure am lucky he wasn't radioactive. I'd be stuck with all the attributes of a squirrel. I'd have super-human tree climbing abilities and the uncanny ability to store acorns in secret locations all winter. And those would be the cool powers.

I'd also be in a constant state of jittery anxiety with a strong penchant for running out into traffic.

"Out in the middle of the road!"

"It's a dog!"

"It's a possum!"

"It's Squirrel-boy! And he can't decide which way to run!"

The X-Men are a team of superheroes, but they were all born with super powers through some sort of mutant glitch in their genetic make-up. Storm, for instance, was born with the ability to control the weather, while Magneto has complete control over metal objects.

The same premise posed above must also apply to mutants. There have got to be some really boring mutants out there somewhere - mutants born with super-powers that offer them no advantages whatsoever. You could have been born with the mutant ability to build perfect campfires and at super-human speeds, for example. Sure you'd be a terrific Scoutmaster, but you'd still never get your own comic book.

I know one person whom I suspect really is a mutant. He seems to have the mutant ability to expel bad breath over great distances – even, I suspect, over the phone. I call him Captain Halitosis when he isn't around, but I wouldn't give him his own comic book...unless it was a scratch 'n sniff.

The Louie Hole

My hometown of Wilmington was a great place to grow up.

Of course, there was the trauma of the "Louie Hole" to contend with.

I attended elementary school at the Woburn Street School and started out as a car rider. By fourth grade, I was able to convince my mother to let me walk to school. Most of the other kids in the neighborhood walked, I had argued, and I considered myself to be a very worldly 9-year old. By the time I started walking, all of the veteran "walkers" were well versed in the ways of the Louie Hole.

Directly across the street from the Woburn Street School, by the crosswalk, is a manhole cover. That manhole cover was known to all as the deadly and fearsome Louie Hole. As students waited for the Crossing Guard to let them cross the street, each and every one of them was biting the side of their right index finger – self-inflicted bite marks were the only known inoculation against Louie Hole infection. It must have been an interesting site to drive by 20 or so elementary school children all simultaneously biting down on their index fingers while waiting to cross the street.

The rules were as follows – As you walked past the Louie Hole, you spit on it. If you were foolish enough to inadvertently step on the Louie Hole, you instantly transformed into the despicable "Louie Man." The Louie Man could only get rid of his/her affliction by tagging someone who did not have visible teeth marks on his/her right index finger. Otherwise the Louie Man retained the status of "gross" until some other dolt should happen to step on the manhole cover.

Nobody wanted to be the Louie Man and no one would ever admit to being friends with the Louie Man.

What did I know? Trust me; no one warns you about the Louie Hole and once you step on it everyone around you scatters immediately like birds following a gunshot. When I stepped on it, I had no idea what had just happened. Everyone around me began screaming and running. I was also about to scatter when it became obvious that I was the center of whatever calamity had befallen the group. I was quickly informed by several inoculated kids of my newly acquired identity and of the general rules.

I was indeed in dire straits. Everywhere I turned were fully vaccinated index fingers. Despite their self-administered full-proof protection, I was deemed persona non-gratis by all of my friends. They would have nothing to do with the Louie Man. Even my own sister pretended not to know me and assumed that I had done the whole thing simply to embarrass her.

Luckily, my trauma was short lived. Some really stupid third grader stepped on the Louie Hole the next day. Man, did I ever make fun of that dumb kid.

I have often wondered if the current student body of the Woburn Street School still acknowledges the powers of the Louie Hole.

If they don't, then somewhere out there is a person who still holds the stigma of being the Louie Man; having never been able to get rid of it under the rules of the game. If he is out there somewhere, he is surely planning to purge himself when no one is expecting it. Only people who attended the Woburn Street School would be eligible and that makes me a potential target. I bite my right index finger every single day just to be safe. When the game starts up again, and I have no doubt that it will, I will be ready. I suggest you take precautions also.

Recess

Perhaps the most disappointing element of adult life is the absence of daily recess. I don't know exactly what happened to recess; I just know that no one ever tells me to go to it anymore.

Of course, the recess of today's youth may not have many parallels to the recess of our past. I can't imagine that children today are allowed to do any of the things that we were allowed to do.

Kill The Kid With The Ball was the quintessential recess game. There were no out-of-bounds, there were no rules to argue about...there wasn't even a way to score points.

The game was simple – if you were holding the ball, you were screwed.

For those unfamiliar, the game starts with approximately 50 to 60 fifth-graders standing in a disorganized mob. Whoever brought the Nerf football threw it up in air and as it fell back to the Earth everyone tried to catch it like a bunch of old maids going for the last bouquet of the wedding season.

Whoever happened to catch it went immediately into a full-tilt serpentine sprint around the playground to avoid the throng following close on his heels trying to break his spine. It was not unlike the running of the bulls in Spain.

Eventually the horde of maddened youngsters would catch up to and drag the kid down to the ground by weight of sheer numbers, if not athletic ability. The Nerf would pop up and out of the crowd, an instant before bones started breaking, only to land in the willing hands of the next victim. For some reason we all wanted a chance to outrun the mob.

The cycle repeated itself over and over until the bell rang or until there was a corpse on the playground clutching our beloved Nerf in rigor mortis hands. There was no other definitive way to end the game, at least none that we were aware of.

We loved Kill The Kid With The Ball and could play it for hours, or at least for the full fifteen minutes of the recess period. I remember only one kid who never wanted to play - he was a devout pacifist. We used to chuck the Nerf at him and then gang-tackle him where he stood at least two or three times every recess.

Red Rover was another popular game jam-packed with violence and potential for serious injury. If you were a "husky" kid, Red Rover was your game.

Red Rover typically involved approximately 300 second-graders split up into two groups. Each group stood on opposite ends of the playground with the players of each group standing side by side and facing the opposing team, so that you've basically got two parallel lines of students facing each other.

Each player stretches out his arms and holds onto the hands of the player to each side of him. To be completely accurate, players don't hold on to each other's hand; they grab at the wrist. It is far easier to lose a grip on someone's hand than from someone's wrist, and any player worth his salt would much rather rip his best friend's arm off at the shoulder than risk being the weak-link of the team. If your friend's arm was ripped from his shoulder, well that was his tough luck; you've done your job properly.

The goal of Red Rover is to run through the arms of two players on the opposing team causing them to break their connection. If you fail to break their connection, then you are a big loser and have to stand in their group.

To start the festivities, the leader of one of the groups pulls out a bull horn and yells, "Red Rover, Red Rover, send ... Jimmy right over!"

• • •

From the opposite team, a seven-year old kid from Hell bursts out of his line and sprints towards the opposing team. He is running as fast as his little legs will carry him and all the while he is scanning the opposing team for the weakest link – the anemic kid.

Everyone went to school with an anemic kid. In our school, his name was Gregory.

Gregory was not a big child. He was med-flighted off the playground three days a week.

Most of the kids had mercy and would let him play the game without running at his fragile arms. The poor kid barely had enough energy to stand for the entire recess, never mind staving off 60-pounds worth of angry kid from slamming into his forearm eighty times over the course of a recess. So the unwritten Red Rover etiquette was not to target Gregory. There were some jerks, somewhat lacking in integrity, of course, who did it anyway.

Gregory was a survivor, however. Eventually he developed a failsafe strategy. When he saw that he was being targeted, he'd wait until the no-good kid was inches away and then raise his pitiful limb up a few inches and clothesline his opponent. Gregory's arm would catch right under the chin, sending runner up and over and, rather unceremoniously, head first into the ground.

Concussion, every single time!

I suffered eight concussions before I got wise to Gregory's new move.

The star of Red Rover, in my school, was a kid named Lunchmeat. Lunchmeat was not fast by any measurable standards, but he was big and mean. By fourth grade he was 6'1" and 250 pounds. By sixth grade he had a five-o'clock shadow and was able to purchase alcohol without being carded.

When it came to Red Rover, he never ran for the opponents' arms – he ran straight at the chest of a kid on the opposing team. Nine times out of ten the targeted kid would panic from seeing this Neanderthal-looking freak running straight for him and would break from the line without even being touched.

The only effective strategy to use against Lunchmeat was to put as much space as possible between your team and his. The opposing team would go ahead and call Lunchmeat, who'd break out of his line and subsequently collapse from exhaustion before reaching the other team.

Lunchmeat turned out to be one of those kids who peaked early as far as athletics go. In addition to his vaunted Red Rover skills, he was the best kickball player my elementary school has ever seen; a virtual celebrity for six years. He'd kick a home run every single time he got up to the plate and then he'd do a slow jog around the bases in his brown corduroy pants while the ball bounced around on Route 93 – in Somerville. He would finish rounding the bases and then sign a few autographs for fans who came in from all over the state to see him play.

Unfortunately for him, Red Rover and kickball tend to lose popularity as you move up in the educational system. There is no varsity Red Rover team at the high school level and there are no Big Ten colleges recruiting all-star kick-ballers. For this he was eternally bitter and he still recounts the glory days of his kickballing years for any who will listen.

Lunchmeat tried soccer, but he tended only to be good for about one kick per day. He also gave football a try, but alas, it was a sport requiring movement and stamina.

Perhaps the most dangerous of all elementary school games was Dodgeball. Dodgeball was truly insidious, because it was played in gym class under the "supervision" of the gym teacher and participation was required. Gym teachers are sick individuals. Gym classes were co-ed in elementary school, and there was no mercy offered to the fairer sex.

Dodgeball and kickball, incidentally, were the only known uses for that red, textured vinyl ball from gym class. There is nothing else to do with that ball. You'll never see another one of them post-elementary school graduation.

The object of Dodgeball, if you were on the outside, of course, was to peg everyone in the middle. The objective for those in the middle was to live another day; by not being beaned in the skull by the 10-pound Dodgeball.

The texture on the ball was useful for resolving Dodgeball discrepancies.

"Get out of the middle; I hit you with the ball," the kid on the outside would say to the cheating liar in the middle.

"You did not hit me. You totally missed me!" the no-good cheater would say.

"Then why are those crisscross lines imprinted all over your stupid face?!"

Then I'd have no choice but to leave the middle area.

There was, we found out in our seventh grade phys-ed class, a step up from Dodgeball.

Bombardment!

The gym teacher had the whole class spread out and standing against the walls of the gym on Bombardment day. He'd walk into the center of the gym, empty a bag full of Dodgeballs and then run like the dickens for cover.

With a legitimate fear of death urging us on, every member of the class would dash towards the center to grab a ball. If you were quick enough, you got a hold of a ball to hurl at any one else in the class. If you were a tad too slow, you found yourself quickly turning tail only to get nailed right in the back of the head.

Bombardment was a beautiful chaos. Within seconds of the balls being dumped out of the bag, noses were bleeding and thick-rimmed eyeglasses were flying through the air all over the place.

Those were good times.

Shaking Hands

When two men greet, there is usually a handshake involved. Sounds fairly innocuous, but I've found there to be a wide range of hand-shaking techniques - many of which continue to confuse me.

Let's start with the basics – The "Insurance Man" technique is the one that people are probably most familiar with. It involves the standard grip, with the webbing located between the thumb and index finger of your right hand meeting the same webbing of your subject's right hand, followed by a firm grasp and some general shaking back and forth.

Sounds simple doesn't it? So, how does it get screwed up so badly so often?

Some people insist on closing their hand before appropriate web-connection has been established, thereby leaving you to stand there like a simpleton as they excitedly shake the ends of your four fingers up and down.

Other people use the "Crab-Claw" variation of the Insurance Man technique. In this case, no attempt at web connection is made. Instead of wrapping their hand around yours, the tips of their four fingers press on the middle of your palm while their thumb presses on the back of your hand. I hate that one.

The simplest handshake can go awry even when proper technique is utilized. I hate it when the other person won't let go within any normal passage of time. We start out in a formal, yet masculine greeting; sharing pleasantries and all, and the next thing I know the shake is all over, but somehow he's still got a hold of my hand. That's an uncomfortable situation. Suddenly I'm standing there intimately holding hands with some guy that I wasn't even sure I wanted to shake hands with.

That guy is closely related to the dreaded "Incessant Shaker." This nimrod is so excited to see you and to shake your hand that he just keeps shaking your hand violently throughout the conversation and then dinner. Finally, you break away just in time to get your torn rotator cuff looked at.

Here's a general rule – three shakes and be done with it. Don't prolong it for God's sake.

No matter what else happens, please, in the name of all that is sacred, give me a firm handshake. I hate going in for a handshake and getting a soft, limp hand. It's an insult and it is disturbing. It feels like I'm shaking a dead squid.

How about people with sweaty palms? Is that gross, or what? You stick your hand in with authority and end up squeezing a fistful of tapioca pudding. It's not so bad when they do the courtesy pants-rub with their palm immediately before contact. At least then you have some warning and can brace for it.

The second most popular basic technique is the "Soul-Man" technique, during which each person's arm is held in an arm-wrestling position and the right hands meet by wrapping around each-other's thumb. This technique is often accompanied by various levels of hootin' and hollerin' and is extremely popular amongst carnival workers and professional wrestlers.

The "Soul-Man" technique can be finished with exotic hand-choreography and tribal dance steps.

All other handshakes invariably begin with some variation of the "Insurance Man" or "Soul Man" techniques, and some people will actually give you the combo package. They start out with the "Insurance Man" and then deftly transition into the "Soul Man," resulting in the oft attempted, but seldom perfected "Soul Loving Insurance Man" technique. This technique is generally tolerated amongst teenagers, but grown men who attempt this technique have generally spent too much time watching Ace Ventura movies all by themselves.

The "Shake-N-Pull" technique has gained some popularity in recent years among adult males. It generally begins with a standard "Soul Man," but the initial shake is then used as a means to draw the other party into a one-handed back-slapping hug. The "Shake-N-Pull" is often accessorized with affectionate shouts of, "Where you been hiding?" or "Whatchu been up to?" or "Congratulations on your new monster-truck!"

Be advised, incidentally, that hugs between straight men must always include a firm pat on the back. No exceptions. If your friend has lost a loved one or has dropped the very last bottle of beer, it is acceptable to offer a hug, so long as only the chest and arms touch and it is finished off with a minimum of three quickly administered one-handed back-slaps from both participants during the break. It is never okay to melt into your buddy's arms nestling your head on his shoulder.

The "Two-Hander" is especially effective at wakes and in hospitals. It begins with the classic "Insurance Man," but with your left hand coming in a moment later, gently covering both hands in a comforting manner. For the full effect, an empathetic look and a slow subtle nodding of the head is recommended. Experts in this technique will throw in a slight sigh and a softly spoken, "How are you holding up?"

If done effectively, your subject will signal approval of the technique by covering your left hand with his/her left hand and mimicking your slow nodding movement.

The "Shake-N-Kiss" is often used to greet close friends of the opposite sex as well as those aunts you only see once a year.

Be warned - the "Shake-N-Kiss" is undoubtedly the most dangerous of all handshakes. Typically starting with the "Two-Hander," both parties lean in for a kiss on the cheek. Be damn sure you are able to ascertain which cheek your subject is going for. Read it wrong and you'll find yourself locking lips with 72-year old Aunt Edna smack dab in the middle of the funeral home. That's not a comfortable situation for anyone in the room, I assure you.

And then, the next thing you know Aunt Edna's number keeps showing up on your caller ID at all hours of the night and you have to go through the hassle of changing your phone number and getting a restraining order. Aunt Edna never learns.

Want to have some fun? Insist on shaking with your left hand. People have no idea how to react to that. Eight times out of ten they will wear an expression of confusion and, after a moment of uncertainty, will proceed to shake your left hand as best they can with their right hand. They look completely stupid and, let's face it, that's the whole point, isn't it?

When you get bored with that, try out the "Shake-N-Kiss" technique on your boss at work. This is especially effective if you work in the construction industry.

The Miracle Sandwich

The best story to have come around in the last decade has got to be the ten-year-old half a grilled cheese sandwich that sold for $28,000 on eBay.

That's right - 28,000 bucks...and there was a bite missing from it. It wasn't even a whole half. If you extrapolate that figure out to reflect the worth of the whole sandwich, you're looking at roughly a $56,000 lunch, plus the cost of potato chips and maybe even a Cup-A-soup.

The high cost of the decade-old sandwich is likely due to the fact that a distinctly visible image of a woman appears on one of the grilled pieces of bread. The sandwich's creator, Diana Duyser of Florida, swears it is the image of the Virgin Mary.

"I made this sandwich 10 years ago," Duyser says in the eBay item description. "When I took a bite out of it, I saw a face looking up at me. It was the Virgin Mary staring back at me, I was in total shock."

Duyser had apparently maintained enough of her faculties to throw the other half of the miracle sandwich down her gullet, since its whereabouts are not accounted for. I'd really like to know whose image adorned that other half.

I, personally, see no compelling evidence that the image is that of the Virgin Mary, as opposed to some other random saint. The image, as a matter of fact, looks suspiciously like a 1930's glamour shot of Hollywood star Fay Wray.

Why would the Blessed Virgin Mary show herself on, of all potential mediums, a grilled cheese sandwich? I would be more willing to believe in its authenticity if the image showed up on a lamb chop, or maybe even in the middle of a pâté at a big Christmas Eve dinner party. Or even on a 6-year old child's PB&J during lunchtime at a Catholic school, but a grilled cheese sandwich? Where's the symbolism?

I'm not attacking anyone's faith; if anything I'm attempting to defend it. Those who truly believe in the Bible can surely see the inherent dangers of assuming that a 10-year old sandwich actually contains such a miraculous visage. If the Lord was upset at Moses' people for praying to a Golden Calf, can you imagine how He would react to a bunch of half-wits kneeling before a decrepit sandwich emblazoned with a picture of Mae West.

True; sandwiches are not specifically mentioned in the Bible as false idols, but it is most assuredly implied.

Duyser says that her life has been blessed since the immaculate grilling of the sandwich. She submits, as proof of the sandwich's divine nature, that she has won a total of $70,000 over the past ten years at a nearby casino. Well, that is a rather convincing argument. It is a documented historical fact that the Virgin Mary was a big fan of casino gambling and was a regular at Caesar's Palace (not the one in Vegas, of course).

All of the sandwich-miracles must have sort of dried up recently. I can only surmise that the Duyser family has been on one heck of a losing streak lately; hence the sale of the very item that had purportedly brought them so many blessings.

According to Duyser, the Holy sandwich has not formed any mold and has not degraded in any way over the last ten years, despite no effort on her part to preserve it.

"The item has not been preserved or anything," Duyser says in the eBay item description. "It has been kept in a plastic case, not a special one that seals out air or potential mold or bacteria, it is like a miracle. It has just preserved itself which, in itself, I consider a miracle."

I have to admit, by the way, that I cleaned up some of the spelling and punctuation on Duyser's item description. She obviously didn't invest any of that ill-gotten 70-grand on spell-check software.

Whether the sandwich is a product of divine intervention or not, $28,000 is a lot of dough for a decade-old half-sandwich with one bite missing. It got me thinking. I can be a tad bit forgetful; perhaps I have an unintentionally discarded ten-year-old sandwich lying around the house somewhere. A ten-year-old sandwich with no mold bearing any image – religious or not - must be worth a few bucks.

I tore the house apart and looked everywhere. I searched in nooks and crannies of my house that I hadn't paid any attention to in years, like the shower, hoping and praying to find, maybe, a Rueben on dark rye with an image of Ben Affleck or even an old discarded fried egg sandwich boasting a resemblance to Rosie O'Donnell.

But, alas, my wife is far too fastidious to allow for anything of the sort. The best I could find was a two-week old chicken finger that I had left languishing on my workbench when I heard the ice cream truck. The stupid chicken finger didn't look like anyone.

Undaunted, I used a paring knife to carve a miniature replica of Leonardo da Vinci's Last Supper on the chicken finger and then put it up on eBay with claims that the famous work of art miraculously appeared on the chicken finger when it came out of the fryolator.

So far I have only one bid of five bucks from some guy named "Fraud Division." I'm thinking that I might go ahead and bid on the chicken finger myself just to see if I can get that idiot to up his bid.

Kids Parties

I've been to several kids' parties lately and the majority of them, to my surprise, have involved piñatas.

No more musical chairs. That's too bad. Remember that warm feeling of abject isolation you felt when the music stopped and there was no chair left for you? That was character building.

Okay, sure, pin-the-tail-on-the-donkey may have been a tad bit dangerous. Let's face facts; it is generally not a good policy to allow a blindfolded 5-year old with hypertension run around with a sharp tack.

"Uh-oh, Timmy just pinned the tail on Grandma."

So then, what sense does it make to replace that scenario with a dizzy, blindfolded five-year old child sporting Attention Deficit Disorder and a baseball bat smashing the bejeesus out of a cardboard donkey?

When exactly did piñatas begin monopolizing these parties, anyway? I never saw one when I was a kid and I went to my fair share of parties. It must have something to do with North American Free Trade Agreement.

Just what sort of lesson does a piñata teach children? Let's break it down. The ultimate goal is to smash the piñata repeatedly with a blunt object until it completely breaks apart.

"Children, today we are going to learn the proper way to cause malicious destruction of property. Who wants to go first?"

And we wonder why teenagers go around smashing mailboxes? We encouraged it. These confused teenagers are going to keep smashing our mailboxes until they find one with some damn candy in it.

• • •

Once the piñata has been broken and all of the candy comes pouring out, the children are encouraged to barge through the crowd, pushing and shoving, and grab as much of the goodies as possible. Just a bunch of miniature looters going to work.

Meanwhile, you've got 600 hundred moms and dads cheering the whole thing on.

"C'mon Jimmy! Bash that thing to smithereens! Go for the head! Smash it in the head!"

That, at any rate, is how a piñata is supposed to work, but it never goes quite that well.

My niece has a birthday party coming up next week and she has a piñata every year. Her dad doesn't have a good tree to hang the piñata from, so he ties it to the end of a 6-foot pole and holds it out over the kids.

The birthday girl gets the first turn of course. Kids are huddled all around behind her and with her first backswing she takes out 20 kids - the bulk of the competition.

The kids always start out wearing a blindfold. They're spun around three times and sent off in the vague direction of the worried piñata. The blindfold goes right out the window once Dad has been smashed in the crotch three or four times.

Each kid gets a turn, but they're using a stupid little plastic broom stick while the piñata appears to be made out of titanium steel, so they don't even make a dent in it. After three or four turns, little stragglers begin wandering off aimlessly looking for Hoodsies.

As soon as each of the kids has suffered either a concussion or a torn rotator cuff the game comes to an end.

Out comes the cake and ice cream to replenish the kids' sugar levels.

Dad is supposed to be videotaping his daughter blowing out the candles, but he is busy out in the driveway running over the piñata with his car. He spent $20 on that damn piñata and, by God, he is going to get that thing open.

* * *

Meanwhile, the birthday girl has covered the cake with saliva while blowing out the candles and everyone wants a frosting flower. Mom is doing long division in her head to figure out how to evenly divide three flowers between 314 screaming kids. She'd like some help, but Dad has taken the piñata down to the basement. We can hear the table saw.

Now it's present time.

Kids always go for the biggest present first, but an obstacle stands in the way. An envelope is taped to it. Why do grown-ups buy cards for little kids? For a kid too young to read, a birthday card is like a disciplinary time-out. It's an immovable object standing between the kid and unmitigated bliss. Mom steps in to read the card, essentially bringing the whole merry process to a halt. Dad could read the card, but the sounds of a chain saw and various profanities are now emanating from the basement.

The card is always far longer than it needs to be. Y'know what the card should say? "Here's a big present. Quick, open it."

The party tends to wind down after the presents are opened. The kids are wandering around twitching and grinding their teeth from sugar overload and the parents begin getting ready to leave when they spy Dad standing on the roof of his two story house holding the piñata and laughing maniacally.

He hurls the piñata, which lands with a thud on the cement patio and bursts open splattering candy all over the yard.

The kids are completely unfazed and nonchalantly begin picking up the candy while the Fire Department shows up with the ladder truck to help Dad down from his roof.

Every year we thank the firefighters and offer them cake and ice cream. Every year they smile and politely decline while slipping Dad into a "special" jacket. He just keeps muttering, "Pinata, dead. Pinata, dead," as they close the ambulance door and take him away.

Superheroes Have Domestic Issues Too

Back in 2004, I came across one of the most entertaining new stories I've ever seen.

My schedule had become extremely hectic at the time, because I'd recently begun studying law. Then, as the Judge Mathis show broke for commercial, a breaking news report showed video of a man dressed as Batman standing on a ledge of Buckingham Palace after having scaled the palace's front wall.

Batman, it was reported, is a member of "Fathers 4 Justice," an organization devoted to campaigning for the expansion of rights of divorced fathers to see their children. Who knew Batman had so many problems at home?

He stood on the ledge for more than five hours doing little more than pacing back and forth over a banner reading "Super Dads of Fathers 4 Justice" and occasionally waving at the crowds below. It looked an awful lot like the Caped Crusader was a superhero without a plan.

And may I say, incidentally, that I was very disappointed in Batman's general build. The comic book and the movies apparently go to extremes to exaggerate his overall physique by depicting him in a skin tight costume accentuating every bulging muscle. In real life, however, he appears rather soft and non-athletic with an ill-fitting suit that tends to hang off of him like a baggy prison-issued jumpsuit. The suit was skin-tight in only one area, causing me to avert my eyes and leaving me to wish that he had invested in a codpiece. Holy hotdogs, Batman! Why don't you cover that thing up? No judge in his right mind would allow this guy to see anyone's kids, never mind his own, after seeing him in that outfit.

Police finally removed the Dark Knight Detective from the ledge with a cherry-picker. How humiliating is that for a superhero? Proof positive that he is way past his prime as a crime fighter. In his day, Batman has faced the likes of the Joker, The Riddler, Cat-Woman, and has cheated death on countless occasions. There is no way in the world that he would have fallen for the old cherry-picker trap when he was on top of his game.

On the way down, police removed the Batman mask and replaced it with a white helmet while Batman waved and clapped – apparently more than comfortable wearing a helmet in public.

Now, I'm all for father's rights, but there are circumstances in which a child is better off without the influence of his or her biological father. A dad dressing up as a superhero for the express purpose of scaling a national monument would, in my book, qualify as a textbook example of just such a circumstance. My opinion on this matter could possibly be swayed if the superhero in question was actually foiling a crime as opposed to committing one.

Batman's secret identity, it turns out, is Jason Hatch, a 33-year old father of two who has not been able to see his children in four years, "even though he lived only a short walk away from them," according to Associated Press reports.

Look, if the location of the Batcave is such a big secret, how do you expect the kids to visit?

The story keeps getting better.

Apparently, another Father 4 Justice member dressed as Batman's youthful companion, Robin, accompanied Hatch to the grounds of Buckingham Palace. The two of them used an aluminum Bat-ladder to scale the palace wall, but Robin only made it half-way up. Apparently police considered it out of the ordinary for two superheroes to be climbing up the side of the royal palace in such a fashion and rushed over to the scene.

Robin came right down when police threatened to shoot him. What a wuss! Not until he reached the ground did he come to understand that police in England do not carry firearms.

This is great – Robin, whose secret identity is David Pyke, was not detained by police and was allowed to wander off. Ya gotta love those English Bobbies.

Pyke was quoted as saying, "Not seeing your children is worse than being put in prison." I wonder how he would compare it with being committed to an inpatient psychiatric unit.

Naturally, I assumed that these were nothing more than two nutcases making a mockery of a well-intentioned organization, but after doing a little bit of research I found that this whole Batman fiasco was sanctioned by Fathers 4 Justice and that this was not the first time that superheroes have taken a British landmark hostage in the name of that organization.

According to their website, the organization is a new civil rights organization comprised of fathers, mothers, grandparents, teachers, doctors, company directors, policemen, barristers, and - apparently - superheroes.

In February 2004, for instance, four dull-witted superheroes climbed Bristol's Clifton Suspension Bridge and remained there for an entire day. Batman, Superman, Spiderman, and the Green Arrow stood atop the bridge milling around with little to do. The Green Arrow guy appeared a little bit miffed that all the best heroes had already been spoken for.

When darkness fell they began tossing fireworks off of the bridge; you know, just to add credibility to their general mental state.

There was a great video showing Anna James, a BBC reporter, reporting from the scene. It is dark out and the sounds of fire crackers or M-80's being tossed off the bridge can be distinctly heard in the background.

"We lost one of the superheroes within the last hour," James reports. "He climbed down, managed to evade any notice or arrest from the police, he removed his Superman costume and left the bridge apparently unnoticed even though he was apparently only wearing boxer shorts and a pair of socks."

That's spectacular.

Then in May of 2004, one of their members, disguised as a mild mannered non-superhero, made his way into the House of Commons and struck Prime Minister, Tony Blair, with a paintball.

The group claims that their membership increases dramatically after each of these stunts. I don't find that to be all too surprising. Jim Jones found 900 people to follow him to Guyana and talked them all into drinking poisoned Kool-Aid. No, I'm not surprised that a number of deranged fathers living on the fringe of reality are coaxed into signing up after such stunts, but I would recommend a thorough screening of these recent applicants.

Can you imagine a grown man with a shred of sanity being convinced to join the organization based on those ridiculous antics? Were these new recruits on the fence about the whole thing or did they just happen to have a superhero fetish?

"Welcome to Fathers 4 Justice. We are now in the middle of a letter writing campaign to our representatives in Parliament for extended father's rights."

"Can I be Aquaman while I write my letter?"

"We would expect no less, from you. You, my friend, will fit in very well around here."

How did they come up with the whole superhero idea? What was the runner up option?

"Okay, welcome to the Fathers 4 Justice meeting here in our secret lair. We have two proposals on the table to increase our exposure. Stanley, here, proposes that we draft a petition calling for more rights for divorced fathers to have access to their children and that we canvas the countryside collecting signatures. So far that has received a rather lukewarm reception from the membership. Jason, however, and I have to admit that I'm excited about this one; proposes that we take on the identities of superheroes and make general nuisances of ourselves."

"Maybe we can wear superhero costumes while collecting signatures for the petition?"

"No, I don't think so – it's one or the other, guys. Everyone in favor of shaming our families on an international scale? Great; it's unanimous."

When I first discovered this story I was leaning against the whole Fathers 4 Justice strategy, but I think I've been talked into it. If anybody needs me, I'll be on top of Town Hall in my Green Lantern costume. Yes, I have one; so what?

Werewolves of Wilmington

I saw a werewolf with a Chinese menu in his hand
Walking through the streets of Wilmington in the rain
He was looking for the place called Royal Dynasty
Going to get a big dish of beef chow mein
Werewolves of Wilmington

Strange and unexplained events taking place here in Wilmington during the wee morning hours of mid-autumn.

It must have been about two-ish on Sunday morning when the preternatural animalistic noises first cut through the chill night air. Guttural desperate sounds of furious confinement welling up and exploding from the inner depths of some great tormented beast. My skin went dead cold. My mind raced in futile efforts to link the detestable sounds to any type of species of known animal.

The disturbing noises went on for quite some time and I finally peeked out my window to see my next door neighbor running in circles around his yard like some kind of freak. All of the lights in his house were off, but I could make him out fairly clearly by the light of the full moon. I'm really not one to judge, but he didn't appear to have a whole lot of clothes on for such a cool autumn night and he is most definitely the hairiest Irish dude I've ever seen.

I must have been real tired. As a general rule, it is time to go to bed when you could swear that you've just seen your next-door neighbor leap 20 feet into a tree and eat a squirrel with one quick bite. This particular neighbor has been to many a barbeque at my house and I can attest to his not being a picky eater, but neither has he ever exhibited the slightest indication of a penchant for raw squirrel meat. It was late; I must have been seeing things, so I went to bed.

I chalked the whole thing up to a funky dream by the time I awoke. I did, oddly enough, find approximately 15 of the most massive piles of dog-mess I'd ever seen scattered all across my front lawn. I don't know which one of my neighbors recently obtained a Great Dane, but I do believe there is a pooper-scooper law in this town.

I was pushing my second wheelbarrow load of the stuff towards my backyard garden when I spied my neighbor watching me out of his window. Was that a look of guilt I saw on his face?

Suddenly it hit me. All of a sudden the whole situation became as clear as a teenager's face after a couple of visits to the dermatologist.

My neighbor had become a werewolf.

It must be so embarrassing for his family. Can you imagine having to explain to your friends why your dad sheds all over the sofa whenever there's a full moon? It's the kind of thing that no one wants to admit to and no one ever talks about, but they say it can happen to anyone.

Even a man who is pure at heart
And says his prayers at night
May become a wolf when the wolfbane blooms
And the Moon is full and bright.

See, that's why it's best to say your prayers in the morning and to stay as far away from wolfbane as possible. I have no idea what wolfbane looks like, but it sounds like nasty stuff.

Well, it didn't look like anyone else was willing to tackle the situation head-on, so, as usual; it was apparently going to be up to me.

According to the old movies, there was always an ample supply of silver bullets in Europe during the nineteenth century, but they seem to have fallen completely out of favor, because I couldn't find them anywhere. I even contacted the television studio that use to produce the Lone Ranger series, but they claimed to have no leftovers at all. The term "Silver Bullet" is often used to refer to Depleted Uranium Ammunition, but I found it impossible to get my hands on any of that stuff either.

In the Universal Studios' 1941 Wolf Man release, the monster is killed by being beaten with a silver-handled cane, so I went out and picked up one of those numbers.

For the next week, on a fairly regular basis, I waved the cane at my neighbor in an exceedingly threatening manner while screaming profanities. This resulted in his taking out a restraining order on me, which naturally I fought. How in the world am I supposed to kill a werewolf if I'm not allowed within 100 yards of him? But the judge wouldn't hear, "any of this ridiculous talk of werewolves."

I found the judge's statement especially ironic since my neighbor had repeatedly and feverishly locked onto his leg throughout the proceedings.

When the judge started suggesting I submit to evaluation at McLean Hospital, I decided to pull back. I laid low for the next couple of weeks and just waved my cane arbitrarily out my front door every once in a while.

Then late last night the sounds started up again.

I was ready.

I grabbed my cane and ran out the front door to see my neighbor squatting on my front lawn. Adrenalin and the instinct for self-preservation completely took over and I don't exactly remember the events of the next several moments, but I can tell you that I beat on him pretty good. I treated him like he was a Nissan Altima rented under someone else's credit card.

• • •

To my chagrin, it turned out that he was not a werewolf at all, just a really weird guy.

Now that I think of it, I guess it was my other neighbor that had previously been making all of those noises. Live and learn, I guess, but you can never be too careful with werewolves. My other neighbor had better watch his step.

I saw a werewolf drinking a pina colada at Tremezzo's
His hair was perfect
Werewolves of Wilmington again

Of Mice and Soup

According to a June 2, 2004 report by the Associated Press, a mother and son team was arrested and charged with conspiracy to commit a felony and the attempted extortion of the fine people at a Cracker Barrel restaurant in Newport News, Virginia.

The AP report states that the woman claimed to have found a mouse in her soup while celebrating Mother's Day at the ill-fated Cracker Barrel and subsequently attempted to shake down the company for some dough - to the tune of $500,000.

"The discovery prompted the 500-store chain to stop serving vegetable soup nationwide, but a company investigation discovered the mouse did not originate from the Cracker Barrel kitchen," the AP reported.

My compliments, first of all, to Cracker Barrel for reacting the way that they did. A mouse is not a vegetable and should never be found in a vegetable soup – it defeats the whole purpose. Hell, if it was beef minestrone, it wouldn't be so bad.

Apparently, these two troublemakers brought their own dead mouse to the restaurant and then dropped it into the soup. Sounds to me like they had it planned in advance.

According to the story, the woman claimed to have already eaten some of her soup before discovering the mouse. That leads to one of two conclusions – either the son had no way of paying for the Mother's Day feast and slipped the mouse into mom's soup without her knowledge, or she knew about the mouse and showed an incredible amount of commitment, not to mention intestinal fortitude, to the scam.

I really enjoy the fact that the perpetrators are a mother and son team and that it occurred on Mother's Day weekend. Let's, just for fun, assume it was Junior - who was listed as being 20-years of age - that came up with the full-proof plan.

"Mom, you taught me everything I know and you've made me into the man that stands before you today. Happy Mother's Day. I've got a dead mouse – let's go to Cracker Barrel."

What glorious maternal pride that woman must have felt.

The story takes a rather disturbing twist when the rodent's cause of death was determined by CSI to be a result of foul play.

"We learned that the mouse died from a fractured skull before it entered the soup," Cracker Barrel spokeswoman Julie Davis was quoted as saying.

So now, not only are these two appearing guilty of being con-artists, they have shown an alarming propensity for violence. What do you say when you "whack" a mouse for such a purpose?

"You are going to be sleeping with the oyster crackers."

Killing the mouse ahead of time was definitely their downfall. Man, are they stupid. Everyone knows you have to bring a healthy mouse with you (tell him he is going to get a piece of the score) and then drown him in your soup when the waiter isn't looking.

Well, everyone makes mistakes. I myself was once caught trying to pull off a similar job, but I got the whole thing backwards. I poured lentil soup all over a mouse at the pet store and claimed I found him that way. I demanded a mere $200,000, but nobody was willing to pay and I'm not allowed to go to that pet store anymore.

What really made it rough was when Jim Sokolov took the mouse's case and sued me for everything I had.

The truth is, I've never been very good at crime. With the price of gasoline on the rise, I had heard about a recent proliferation of "Pump & Runs" occurring around the country. I figured I would give it a try, but apparently you are supposed to pump the gas and then leave without paying. Every station I went to had a pay-first policy, so I ended up paying and running before pumping my gas.

This went on for a full week before I figured out why I kept running out of gas and money.

In other news, the AP reported on July 6th that female rice farmers in southwestern Nepal are tending to their crops in the nude because they have been told that it would please the rain god and would end the dry spell.

According to Expedia.com, a last minute ticket from Boston to Katmandu, Nepal runs about $5,113.

If this, so-called, rain god is truly pleased by the prospect of naked female farmers, then why would he make it rain? Once it rains, the women put their clothes back on, right? How stupid do they think this rain god is?

The AP quoted a 35-year old female farmer (who likes long walks on the beach and sincere people, but is really turned off by people who don't believe in rain gods) that it was her mother-in-law's idea. Her mother-in-law deserves a round of applause.

Forecasters in Katmandu are predicting that the weather should improve in the next few days, but did not make any specific suggestions on whether or not it was safe for the female farmers to return to full farming attire.

Beware of Schnozzels

You gotta have fun, even at the expense of others.

Everyone, with the notable exception of the victim, loves a good practical joke and I have personally found small children to be especially easy and satisfying targets.

I would like to pass along a great idea for a practical joke that you can try at your next family barbeque. I tested this during my own Memorial Day cook-out and it went off without a hitch.

To pull this off you will need a minimum of three small children, or perhaps dimwitted adults, and several common household items; such as a small stuffed animal, 3-feet of string, a baby monitor, and an animal hole of some sort in your yard. I just happen to have a hole in my backyard made by a small, burrowing animal, but don't hesitate to dig a hole for the express purpose of this joke. It is worth it.

We had the grill going and people were milling about when the hole was discovered by my 6-year old niece and her 4-year old twin brothers.

"What lives in that hole, Unk?" they asked with eyes wide.

The entire prank hinges on this moment. Yes, you could wimp-out and tell them that a cute little furry animal, such as a chipmunk or maybe a rabbit lives very cozily in the hole, but c'mon; what fun is that?

"A schnozzel lives in that hole," I told them.

That's about all it takes to get this joke off the ground. Then all the questions start flying in from all directions pertaining to the appearance, habits, and general demeanor of schnozzels.

A schnozzel, I explained, is a bluish-grey furry creature, about a foot long with a bushy tail, short legs, and very sharp teeth. Its two front teeth stick straight out in front of it so that it can spear its prey just by running right at it. It is a vicious and vile creature that hates people and especially children. Many a child has had the back of their legs stabbed by nasty schnozzels.

Just to be perfectly clear, there is no such thing as a schnozzel. I made the whole thing up for the joke. You should know that right up front. Feel free to change the story to suit your audience, but don't lay it on too thick yet. Scare them too much too early and curiosity is replaced by terror and you can just forget about the rest of the joke. My niece and nephews weren't sure whether I was kidding or not, which is the best possible scenario.

They were fascinated by the hole and each of them attested to never having seen a schnozzel before in their whole lives. They walked slowly around the hole and tried to peer inside from safe distances. The questions never stopped.

"Yes," I told them, "a schnozzel could definitely beat up a Tyrannosaurus Rex in a fight."

The kids were leery, but desperately wanted to see a real live schnozzel. I suggested that we set-up a Schnozzel Trap to see if he was home. I tied a small stuffed mouse; a cat toy really, to a long piece of string and lowered it far enough into the hole so that it could not be viewed from the outside. I told the kids that we could check back on it in about an hour or so.

Children are easily distracted and while their parents and my wife kept them occupied, I grabbed the stuffed mouse and brought it into the house. After shredding it with a razor blade, I discreetly put it back into the hole and then casually suggested that we check the bait.

My niece pulled on the string until what was left of the mouse came jumping out of the hole like some low-budget horror flick. The kids were beside themselves. Their jaws hit the floor as they stared in disbelief at the eviscerated mouse.

"There really is a schnozzel!" exclaimed one of the twins with his head in his hands.

There was no longer any doubt. Schnozzels were real and most definitely dangerous.

The day was still young, so a little bit later I went into the house and grabbed the baby monitor out of the closet.

For those of you without children; a baby monitor is a device very similar to a walkie-talkie, but only one end transmits and the other end receives. The transmitting end is placed in the infant's room and picks up any and all sound being made anywhere in the neighborhood and transmits it, with a convenient volume enhancement of approximately 1000-times, to the wireless-speaker portion being "monitored" by the parents.

For the dads out there; a baby monitor is that annoying thing that drowns out the sound of your television at night.

I hid the receiving end inside the hole and covered it with leaves and set up the transmitter in my family room near the window.

Then I watched out the window and waited.

Finally, it happened. All three of them were in close proximity of the dreaded schnozzel hole. I made some pretty impressive growling and roaring noises into the transmitter.

Everyone is familiar with the term, but have you ever actually seen a small child "freak-out"? I never had.

The kids were running around at top speed in circles, hiding behind adults, and demanding firearms for protection. It was awesome.

I'm not ashamed to admit that I; a grown man, mind you, spent a significant amount of that beautiful sunny day crouched under my family room window waiting for the perfect moment and then emitting all sorts of unspeakably fierce animal noises into a baby monitor – it was all for the kids.

I'd do it again too. I'd do anything for the kids. They loved it and, according to their parents, still reminisce about the "scary" schnozzel nearly every night. It's nice to be able to create life-long memories. Apparently, since that day, the children refuse to sleep in their own beds and will only sleep with their parents, but I'm sure it is an unrelated passing phase. Those kids had a great time.

I have been asked to share the whole story with some very nice people representing the Department of Social Services. I can only assume that they may want to share the joke with other children.

• • •

My Inheritance

I just found out some rather alarming news about my parents.

Apparently, they have not updated their will in several years. According to their current will, I stand to inherit the Wilmington home that, several years ago, they sold and moved out of.

I know the guy who bought the house; Tom. He's a great guy with a nice family and I'd hate to get into a beef with him. I know he's not going to be happy to hear about this but if push comes to shove, what am I expected to do? Abandon my birthright?

Luckily for both me and Tom, my parents are relatively healthy. I've personally invested a significant amount of time and effort into delivering lots of orange juice and multi-vitamins to them since I heard about this rather embarrassing situation.

Aside from their health, they have absolutely no consideration for my concerns, however. They've been flying all over the country, all willy-nilly over mountains and large bodies of water, without the slightest regard to my financial standing. My father, for instance, just got back from Vegas. I have no idea how much of my future money he lost there as he refuses to discuss it with me.

I have been trying to get them to a lawyer to execute a new will, but between my mother's hang-gliding lessons and my father's NASCAR driving schedule I can't seem to get them together long enough. I have yet to find an attorney who will do it for me without their participation either.

Someday, I'll have my revenge. The reading of my own will is going to be an all-day affair. I am going to include everyone I've ever met in my will, especially those people that I don't particularly like. Why? Because when people find out they are going to get something from a will, they take the time to go and find out what it is. Their entire day is ruined if they don't come out of the lawyer's office with a sizable wad of cash.

When I kick the bucket there are a whole lot of things that I can bequeath out of spite.

"I, Stephen Bjork, being of sound mind and body, do hereby bequeath all of my recyclables to the telephone company."

I could leave all of the wastebaskets in my house to my friend Jeff.

You have to be strategic about this. You have to throw in something of value here and there or people give up and leave. For instance, maybe I leave all of the postage stamps that I haven't used to my friend Mark. He'd like that. Then I can stipulate that the empty stamp booklet thing; once the stamps are used up by Mark, goes to Al.

I can picture my attorney reading the terms of the will to the excited and boisterous crowd.

"Stephen considered donating his organs to scientific research, but decided instead that Jim should have them."

Pranks are great, especially when perpetrated from the beyond. For instance; for my wake, I will instruct my attorney to provide a false address to friends, family, and the newspapers. I'm talking really, really false; like not even a funeral home false. I can picture the confused mourners arriving at what they assume is the Steve Bjork wake.

"Are you sure you have the address right, honey?" a confused husband will ask.

"Well, this is what the newspaper said."

"I really doubt that they are holding Bjork's wake at a Chuck E. Cheese."

But they won't be totally sure that it is out of the question either, so the Chuck E. Cheese staff will be treated to a steady parade of mourners in dark garb stepping in, between the hours of 4pm and 7pm, and congregating over by the Whac-A-Mole game before leaving in a frustrated huff.

Those who do eventually find my wake, will find me in an open coffin incorrectly - with my feet up where my head is supposed to be. I'd be willing to pay an extra fee to have the funeral parlor employees tell all the mourners that it was an unfortunate mistake, perpetrated by an employee who was drinking on the job.

Who could blame the poor guy for drinking, though, since I will stipulate in my will that I be waked in a casket with a built-in keg tap. It will be right there on the side so that people can refill their cups while offering their last respects to me.

Those who actually manage to find my wake will be happy they did.

Voicemails

If you are going to leave me a voicemail message, please, for the love of God, be brief.

"Hey, it's Chaz. Call me back. I'm at home."

That, my friends, is a template for *the* perfect voicemail message. It is succinct, yet it contains all pertinent information needed by the recipient. True, he did not leave his last name, but how many "Chaz's" could any one person actually know? One is too many, quite frankly. In some cases, it will be appropriate to leave your last name; like if your name is Bob or Tom or if you were drunk when the two of you met.

The template above clearly instructs the recipient as to the appropriate response – call him back. There is no confusion. Should you jump in your car and drive right over to the house of Chaz?

No, call him.

Should you send Chaz a letter?

No, call him.

Should you call your best friend and demand, in a threatening manner, to know how the Hell Chaz got your unlisted number?

That is an option to seriously consider.

The message even specifies where good ole' Chaz expects to be when the return call is made. Granted, this message implies a certain level of familiarity. Some people may not know where Chaz lives. They may not know that Chaz is 43 and has been steadily pursuing an Associate's Degree since high school and still lives with his parents, but you know all of that because Chaz is your best friend.

People tend to provide far too much information.

"Hey, it's Chaz from the old neighborhood. What's up man? It's been a while. So, I was thinking about maybe going out for a beer tonight and didn't know if you had plans. If you already have plans, maybe I can kind of tag along. I'd really appreciate it, because...well like I said, I don't have any plans tonight and it's Saturday and all. Heh, heh, otherwise it's just another night of watching the Golden Girls with Mom and Dad for the Chaz-man. Know what I mean, buddy? And listen, it won't be like last time, I swear. So, anyways, I should be at home at 978-555-2222. Alrighty, then. I guess I'll talk to you later. Call me. Take it easy. See you soon."

You are definitely not going to call him back. Too much information.

Are you a chronic long-message-leaver? You might be. There are a number of telltale signs.

Do you find that you have to call back two or three times to complete your message, because the damn machine keeps cutting you off half-way through?

Do you have a $400 cell bill, yet you haven't spoken directly to anyone all month?

Do your friends often begin conversations with, "Hey, what's up? I know you called, but I didn't get a chance to hear your whole message, because I had to (fill in the blank: go to work, go to bed, get an education, etc.)."

Do you find that when your friend does call you back there is nothing left to say?

If you leave every little bit of information possible in your message, what then provides the impetus for a return call? Sometimes a little mystery is the best way to convince someone to call you back.

"Stanley, this is Eustace at the office. We have to talk. Give me a call as soon as you get a chance."

That is a mighty cryptic message for a Friday afternoon. You are definitely going to call Eustace back. What's wrong at the office? Have you been fired? Have you been promoted? Demoted? Has there been some sort of major lay-off?

Turns out, Eustace just needs you to put in a few hours on Sunday afternoon. Since you're on salary, not only are you expected to help out whenever needed, you won't be compensated for it. Had he left all that information on the message, your Sunday would be spent sipping margaritas by the pool instead of sitting beneath stacks of paper in the office.

By, the way, if you reach your friend's voicemail and it makes some weird noise while you are leaving a message – do everyone a favor and hang up. Don't keep asking the machine if your message is being recorded – you just end up sounding like a dolt.

"Hey, Bob. It's Rudabaker here. Call me about the (*squaaaark*) what the…? Hello? Hello? Is this thing still recording? (spoken away from the phone) Bob's voicemail made a weird noise. No, I don't know if it's still recording or not. (back into the phone) Hello? Hey, Bob, so, there was this weird noise and I don't know if you are going to get this message or not, but I was calling you about the thing we talked about before. So…ahh…call me if you get this, but I don't know if you will. Hello? Listen, tell you what; I'll call you right back and leave another message. But if you do get this one don't worry about the other one. Okay? Okay. Bye."

If you hear a weird noise, just hang up the phone and call back. And for God's sake don't talk about the weird noise in your follow-up message. Next time you talk to Bob, go ahead and tell him then. It will make for tremendous conversation.

Let's not forget about the outgoing message that you leave on your own voicemail.

Who still thinks it's cool to play a song in the background while recording their outgoing message? The song starts up and is left on its own for a few seconds and then the imbecile begins speaking. The song is then allowed to play out for another minute after the person stops talking.

People are not impressed; they just think you're a tool.

Outgoing messages do not require as much instruction as they once did. For instance, people are generally aware that they should speak clearly **after** the beep.

This is a common one: "Please leave your name, number, the time of your call and a brief message."

True, some people require more guidance than others; feel free to instruct your dimwitted associates to leave their name and phone number, but do you really need to know what time the call came in? That's a lot of pressure and just one more thing to remember.

"Hi, this is Steve Bjork and my number is 978-555-2222, and it is…oh, cripes my watch stopped. Umm, hold on let me go check the VCR clock. Nope, that one is always blinking. I'll check the kitchen clock so you can have an accurate picture of just exactly what time my call came in. Okay, it looks like it is ten past one in the afternoon. Wait, did we adjust that clock for daylight savings time? I'm not completely sure. It could be ten past two, but it is definitely one of those two times. It is definitely either ten past one or ten past two in the afternoon. We've narrowed it down to those two options. So, anyways, I was calling to tell you (BEEP)."

Great, now I have to call back.

The Doctor Visit

I hate going to the doctor.

The hassle starts as soon as you pull into the parking lot. Good luck finding a parking spot within a mile, unless you are fortunate enough to have some sort of physical disability. I counted 56 handicapped spots in the main lot before succumbing to mental fatigue, so God only knows how many they actually have.

I drove all over the main lot to no avail and then likewise prowled the lower lot with identical failure. Eventually I was lucky enough to find a spot two towns away. By the time I made my way to the building I was lame enough to qualify for disabled parking. Next time I'm just going to park in one of the handicapped spots and then fake a lisp.

The days of a small town doctor or a general practitioner seem to be a thing of the past. Every doctor is a specialist of some sort these days, which seems to me to be little more than an excuse to herd a large number of people with similar ailments together in one waiting room. That way, in the event of a tragedy, the human gene pool may actually improve. I can see it on the 11 o'clock news.

"Early this morning in an, as yet, unexplained tragedy, the roof caved in on the dermatology wing of General Hospital. There were no survivors. In a related story, the medical profession has issued a report this evening indicating a dramatic reduction in the number of reported cases of psoriasis in the state of Massachusetts."

I have asthma, and this appointment happened to be my yearly check-up with my Allergist. So there I was, stuck in a waiting room with a bunch of phlegm-ridden mouth-breathers waiting for a nurse to call my name.

• • •

No one talks to each other in the waiting room. They just spend their time speculating on the potential medical deficiencies of everyone else in the room.

"Check out that guy," they think to themselves with glee. "What a mess. Bet he's allergic to everything. And I wish that other freak would cover his mouth when he coughs."

Ideally, you've remembered to bring something to read, or else you end up choosing between a Newsweek from 1983 or this month's Highlights For Children. Sometimes, regardless of how low your standards are, someone has scooped up the very last copy of Halitosis Monthly leaving you with nothing at all. No one is able to pull off the appearance of being intelligent when sitting in a chair with nothing to read and no one to talk to, just staring out into space.

Finally, the nurse called my name and brought me in to check my weight and blood pressure. I always feel the need to explain that my weight would be far more accurate if I wasn't so overdue for a haircut.

They don't measure my height anymore, which is a real gyp if you ask me. My height I can actually manage to maintain every year.

I really think the blood pressure test is a crock. They pump enough air into the collar to cut off all circulation to your lower arm and hand, and then pretend to listen to the stethoscope while your hand begins to shrink and curl up like a prune from loss of fluid. I'm convinced that they have music pumped into the ear pieces of those stethoscopes.

Now it's time to see the doctor, right? Nope.

Now it's time to wait in a smaller waiting room known as the examining room for three or four days.

"Strip down to the waist," the nurse orders just before closing the door on you.

There you are…all alone…in a little room with a johnny and a table covered in deli paper.

No indication of when the doctor plans on coming in.

No magazines.

Nothing to do.

Maybe the nurse went to lunch and forgot to tell him about you.

This is one of those occasions that women have a distinct advantage over men. At least they get to pass the time away by playing with those stirrup things. Not guys. We have to make due with tongue depressors and that thing that shines light into your ear.

I try to resist every single time. I try to sit there on the paper not touching anything, but if the doctor doesn't show within 15 minutes or so, I just kind of figure it's his fault. No one else who knows me is foolish enough to leave me unsupervised for that long a period of time.

It never fails; the doctor walks in just in time to catch me with a blood pressure collar wrapped around my neck, while trying to look up my own nose in the mirror while using one of those nostril-spreader-things.

My doctor, by the way, always enters the room stripped down to the waist. He does this, he explains, in an effort to ease the discomfort his patients may feel from having to similarly disrobe. Each year I try to convince him that my comfort level would greatly improve if he were to wear a shirt, tie, and maybe even a lab jacket, but he insists that I am just trying to be polite and he really doesn't mind at all, etc, etc. Finally, we compromise and he puts on a johnny.

Oddly enough, I have to endure an almost identical argument with my dentist every six months, but that's a separate story.

New Year's Eve

Here we go once again, headlong into a new year. Once again we celebrated on December 31st and toasted to a New Year. And once again, many sorry souls took down the Christmas decorations while enduring the obligatory New Year's Day hangover.

Well, I would just like to say for the record: Good riddance to the prior year. What a miserable year.

I dared not hold a cookout on the Fourth of July for fear that one of my guests would invariably contract West Nile Virus or suffer exposure to E. coli. Whatever happened to good old fashioned food poisoning?

One thing is for certain year in and year out - people will make New Year's resolutions and most of those good people will break them before the weekend is out.

The only resolution I have ever kept was the one I made in 1998, at which time I resolved not to make any more New Year's resolutions. I now enjoy watching other people try to live up to their resolutions.

My favorites are the smokers. Keep your eyes and ears open on New Year's Eve and you too can enjoy this wonderful pastime. Listen for it and you will hear one or two smokers talking up their intentions to quit, once and for all, on New Year's Eve.

"That's right (exhale smoke). This is the year alright (flicks ashes). I am going to enter the new year (pause in sentence for exhale of smoke) as a bona fide non-smoker (lights a new cigarette with the glowing tip of the filter of his last) and I'm going to stick to it this time. I got the patch, the gum, and one of those vapor things (long drag on new cigarette). I'm gonna get in shape too (exhale...long exhale)."

These people are a lot of fun to watch at the New Year's Eve party, but keep your coat on, because at no time do they actually enter the dwelling. They spend the entire evening out on the porch with the two or three other doomed smokers who also happen to be quitting that night. The cold doesn't bother *them* in the least. After all, the comfy porch is a big step up from leaning against the dumpster outside the office every day. As long as someone comes out periodically to replenish their booze, they will just stand on the porch chain smoking to their heart's content, all the while talking excitedly with each other about how wonderful life will be without "these damned cigarettes."

Keep your eye on them at around 11:45 p.m. when one of them realizes that only 15 minutes of heavenly smoking remains; and he still has a full pack of cigarettes in his pocket. In a panic he starts smoking two and three at a time. Hurriedly inhaling and exhaling; idle conversation and social interaction has become nothing more than an increasing annoyance. The other smokers pick up on the cue and follow suit with their own brands.

I've always found it interesting that smokers would prefer one brand to another. Generic cigarettes, of course, cost significantly less than name brands. Ah, yes, people who choose generics are truly thrifty smokers. Apparently, these people want the associated medical issues, they just don't want to pay for them.

Somewhere, deep down in the fog of secondhand smoke, they take a quick count of their remaining stock and realize that they are not going to make it in time. Moreover, it occurs to them that they may not want to make it.

At 11:58 pm the soon-to-be-reformed smokers go their separate ways; each on a mission to find a "friend" who can be entrusted with the leftover smokes. They pass by all the

• • •

resolved-to-be dieters who are hunched over the table of food, wolfing down last minute Doritos, chips, pastry, and rotisserie chickens.

"Don't give them back to me no matter what I may say," the hapless friend is instructed.

At the stroke of midnight champagne is consumed, lips are kissed, and noisemakers do their thing. Everything is okay for now, but keep your eye on Smokey; it usually takes about five minutes. He will be right in the middle of a conversation with someone, no doubt receiving hearty praise for his fortitude.

His hands begin trembling mildly and his face will almost - but not quite - mask his oncoming panic. He will be restlessly shifting weight from one leg to the other. His hand will make a mad stab into his pocket and come out with five or six pieces of nicotine gum, which he pops quickly into his mouth and begins munching maniacally; lips smacking and smiling bleakly. Still wrapped up in a panic, he will frantically strip down to the waist and apply several nicotine patches to various places on his torso, much to the discomfort of the gathering crowd.

Nothing is working. Nothing is curing this god-awful craving. "Maybe just one more cigarette," he thinks to himself. After all, it isn't really the New Year until the next morning right? All resolutions are null and void until you wake up on New Year's Day right?

After a brief, and one-sided, fist fight - actually the correct term would be 'sucker-punch' - Smokey is able to wrestle the leftover cigarettes from his former friend. Back out on to the porch he happily marches. He is met by the other two smokers and they are all still planning to wake up the next morning as non-smokers.

On his way home he contemplates the agony of taking down the Christmas tree and all the decorations without the comfort of a lit cigarette and he stops for a fresh pack.

Not to worry, there is always next year.

Marco Polo!

Have you seen your children lately? If not, chances are they're in my pool. Please come get them.

I have found that kids will not get out of the pool unless threats of violence are levied against them. I've tried everything else. They don't even get out when empty promises of cake are made.

"C'mon!" I shout every year. "I've got to close the pool, it's December!"

They stay in for hours and hours while their skin gets all pruned up and bleached white from the chlorine. My 6-year old niece has been in my pool for 19 days straight. She's starting to look like Gollum from The Lord of the Rings.

If you've got little kids swimming in your pool, keep this in mind: the Floaties go on the kid's arms, not on the ankles.

My son, now that he is a bit older, has a different modus operandi. He and his friends storm the pool nearly every day with the sole intent of Cannon-balling every drop of water out of it. I'm just sitting there by the pool innocently writing and minding my own business when, without warning, an entire horde of teenagers with towels has descended upon the hapless pool.

Within minutes the pool is empty. I have been involuntarily drenched and am suddenly in need of a new laptop. Disappointed that there is no more havoc to be wreaked in the immediate vicinity, they tie towels around their waists and talk about rap music while herding into my house. In the house, they excel at dripping all over the floor, soaking the furniture and playing X-Box. I'm never sure if they've even noticed my presence at all.

When I was a kid we used to play Marco Polo in the pool for hours and hours.

Marco Polo is a pool-game. Don't look for a description of it on the Internet; a Google search simply comes back with sites about some ancient explorer dude who used to visit some place called Cathay and enjoyed silk or something. There are a lot of sites devoted to that guy, which makes it an unfortunate coincidence that he shares his name with this particular game.

For those unfamiliar with Marco Polo (the game, not the explorer), one person is "it" and can transfer his "it" status to another player by tagging them.

Sounds easy, but wait, there's more.

The "it" person must keep his eyes closed at all times, searching for his opponents solely through the sound of their voices. Whenever the "it" person says "Marco" all of the other players must respond with a resounding "Polo," even if they have secretly moved into the kitchen for cake.

There was a brief time in my life during which I was determined to be the greatest Marco Polo player the world had ever seen. I used to practice all by myself for hours.

"Marco!" I'd shout.

"Polo!" I'd answer.

Then I'd try to tag myself before I could get away, and I would nearly always be successful. I started to get pretty conceited about my Marco Polo abilities and would often brag in the school yard. I soon found, to my utter consternation, that it is a far more difficult game when other people are involved.

Marco Polo (the game, not the explorer) is best played with blind kids, because I have yet to meet one person that didn't cheat. No one admitted it at the time, no matter how damning the evidence, but everyone cheated.

"Hey!" a typical Marco Player would yell when I was a kid. "Your eyes were open!"

"No they weren't!"

"I waved at you underwater and you waved back, ya moron. Play right and take off those stupid goggles."

If you really want an accurate gauge of a person's truthfulness, ask them if they ever cheated at Marco Polo (the game, not the explorer).

"Mr. Clinton, did you ever cheat when playing Marco Polo?"

"I opened my eyes, but I never saw anyone."

"Are you saying that you never actually cheated when you were 'it' during a game of Marco Polo?"

"Well, that depends on what your definition of the word 'it' is."

Adults, sadly, tend not to play Marco Polo. I've tried to initiate games on several occasions and got a "No Tresspass Order" filed against me from the YMCA for my efforts.

Y'know what's fun? Just scream MARCO! at inopportune moments; like right in the middle of the bank or during a job interview.

"Well, you have a very nice background and..."

"Marco!"

"... Excuse me?"

It's even more fun if you are actually conducting the interview. Make a rule that you'll hire the first person that responds with the appropriate, "Polo!"

Here's one that I tried the other day. Burst into the yard of a complete stranger, jump into his pool, right in amongst his whole family, close your eyes and start screaming, "Marco!" If no one responds, yell louder and don't hesitate to become belligerent.

Boy, those are good times.

I found, not long after that stunt, that it is not a good idea to scream, "Marco!" in the middle of a jail cell. Yeah, who knew, right?

Going to the Game

The idea of a father and son outing to a professional sporting event surely does conjure up an idyllic Norman Rockwell-style image.

I picked up a pair of tickets from a friend for the Patriots pre-season opener on Friday night. What fun!

My first mistake was allowing only three hours of travel time for the 45-mile trek down to Foxboro. There we were in the parking lot known as Route 1 South, two miles away from Gillette Stadium at 8:02 p.m. listening to the kick-off on the radio.

By 8:40, I'd had enough. I could see the lights of the stadium and decided to get out of the gridlocked traffic by pulling into one of the hundreds of dirt parking areas littering the side of the road. It would be worth it to part with a few bucks.

Some mutant with a red flag pointed me towards a much bigger mutant standing in the back of the lot. In one hand he had a wad of cash while his other hand was two knuckles deep in his left nostril searching futilely for brain matter. I made a mental note to give him exact change.

"Forty," he grunted into my open window.

"Forty what? Forty dollars?"

"Yeah."

"No, I just want to park here. I'm not trying to sell the vehicle."

Forty it was. Two twenties – exact change. It is difficult to believe that we could still be in the middle of a weak economy when mental deficients like me are willing to fork over $40 to leave a perfectly good automobile in a tire-destroying gravel pit located more than a half-mile from their destination for little more than three hours.

The first quarter of the game was nearly over by the time we started walking.

Within seconds of entering the stadium, the rain began. Wonderful. Things were really looking up. We didn't have an umbrella (see Prohibited Items List on www.gillettestadium.com).

The "friend" who gave me the tickets did mention that they weren't great seats, but I figured, how bad could they be? Well...they weren't good, I'll tell you that much.

They were located in section 316, row 23. To make this clear; the 100 section of the stadium is closest to the field and there is no 400 section. We were in row 23 out of 25 and to add insult to injury, they were end zone seats. Basically, there were only two rows of people in the entire stadium that could possibly be envious of our seats.

From where we were sitting, with the rain pelting down on us, it was impossible to see the football or make out the numbers on the players' jerseys. Hell, from our seats we could barely discern which players were with which team. Finally, my son and I just made an agreement that when the stadium stood up and cheered, we'd go ahead and follow suit. It was kind of like standing and kneeling in church – check out your neighbors for the appropriate cues.

I'm not a prude by any stretch of the imagination, but when I was a kid you could go out in public, including sporting events, without having to listen to profanity. I don't know why people feel like it is okay to just let loose with F-bombs and all kinds of assorted four-letter words in public these days, but it's not okay. And the worst part is it just seems to be accepted by everybody within earshot. It got so bad that I finally had to tell my son to cut it out.

We headed down to the concessions and that's when I let loose with the profanities. A beer, a Coors Light at that, went for $9. That'll straighten out the most fervent of alcoholics. Absolutely outrageous. In protest to such absurd prices, I only purchased eight beers.

Even McDonalds empties your wallet at Gillette Stadium. I paid $20 for two combo meals and we didn't even super-size them. See, they know you are over a barrel as soon as you step foot in the place. You can't bring in your own food (see Prohibited Items List on www.gillettestadium.com) so they figure, $5.50 for a single hot dog is reasonable. $6.00 for a fried dough is okay. $3.50 for a little bag of peanuts is just about right.

Additionally, every concession stand has a tip cup set up, just to rub a little salt into the wound. Sure, you'd like to stab the concession guy, but you don't have a knife (see Prohibited Items List on www.gillettestadium.com).

The fans at home do miss out on the thrilling half-time show, but not us. We were treated to the Levitra football toss in which two middle aged gentlemen threw footballs at targets set up on the field for money.

Maybe it's just me, but do we really need Levitra, Viagra, and all of those other "male enhancement" prescription drugs advertised every fifteen seconds. I don't care about all of the sports figures, celebrities, and political figures who have the "courage" to come forward with their "problem." We don't need to know that these people are back at it again. Tell it to Jerry Springer; at least I have the choice of whether or not I want to watch that program. Enough is enough. It makes one long for the days of being embarrassed by a good old fashioned feminine product commercial.

Scattered throughout the concourse of the stadium during the game are hundreds of dimwits hootin' and hollerin' for no apparent reason whatsoever. I've never understood the desire to do that, but these guys are all over the place.

I can get fired up, and I'll cheer for a good play as loud as the next guy, but I'm referring to the all too common

Neanderthal that just screams and lifts his arm in the air to acknowledge nothing in particular. You can generally see these guys staggering around the concourse in groups of two or three spilling beer on each other. If they are not shirtless, they are wearing a Patriots jersey emblazoned with the name and number of whichever player they happen to have a crush on. All of a sudden, without any sort of prompting at all, one of them will let loose with a bloodcurdling, "Wheeeeeeeewwww!"

What exactly is the purpose of that? Did their conversation hit a lull? Did they just happen to remember that they were at a sporting event? Did the Levitra just kick in?

Look, don't get me wrong – going to the Pats is a great time if you can schedule your entire life and budget around it. If you can get there six hours ahead of time and tailgate with a bunch of people, that's a great time, no doubt about it.

You've also got to be willing to sit out the traffic leaving Gillette Stadium at the end of the game. If you've never seen Route 1 after a Pats game, just imagine what it would be like following an announcement that Seabrook Nuclear Power Plant was melting down and the state needed to be evacuated. Now add to that image the caveat that everyone involved just happened to be drunk at that exact moment.

I'll be watching the next preseason from the best seat in the house. The recliner located deep in the heart of my Man Cave.

My Telephone Number

Why does everyone want my phone number?

I bought three pairs of socks at TJ Maxx the other day - I'm not bragging; it is just part of the story. The total for my socks was $20.97. Okay, okay, I got some underwear too – can we just move on?

I had cash. I held out $21.00, but the cashier wasn't ready to take the money yet.

"What's your phone number?" she demanded.

Why does this lady want my phone number? I'm buying three pairs of socks and some underwear – that offers no basis whatsoever for a meaningful telephone conversation. I couldn't imagine that they might have a customer service department interested in providing a courtesy call a month from now.

"Hello?"

"Is this Mr. Bjork?"

"Yes..."

"How's that underwear working out for you?"

"Pretty good. Who is this?"

"We have a special offer available today only for underwear purchasers. How would you like to purchase a 6-month warranty on those skivvies?"

I have to admit I was caught off guard when the cashier asked and didn't know what to say. I ended up telling her my number was 411. She seemed to be okay with that.

Everywhere you shop these days, they want your phone number so they can put you into their "loyalty programs" and send you useless emails. I really hate that.

Radio Shack started the whole thing back in the 1980's. Of course back then I didn't mind so much. If was going through a bit of a dry spell dating-wise, I'd just cruise various Radio Shack locations for a cute cashier. I'd run in and buy a pack of batteries and boost my confidence up a notch.

"Can I have your phone number, please?"

"Whoa, this is moving a little bit fast for me," I'd say. "Slow down. Let's get to know each other a little bit."

"Aren't you the weirdo that was in here yesterday buying a walkie-talkie?"

"Cut me some slack, it's been a rough winter."

Most people go ahead and give the cashier their phone number, because they just don't want a confrontation, but if you give in on the phone number question and it doesn't show up in their system it simply initiates a whole new series of questions.

Next they want your address and name. Hey, if you've allowed it to go that far you might as well have some fun with it. I give a different phone number every single time I walk into Stop & Shop. They are currently mailing their weekly flyers to me at more than 30 different addresses. Every single work address I've had since I was 14 for instance, is receiving a Stop & Shop flyer in my name, as are most of my closest friends.

I have to admit, it's not easy to refuse their insistent demand for your phone number. I am convinced beyond any doubt that out there somewhere exists some kind of training class instructing all of these cashiers on precisely how to extract customer phone numbers, because they all do it in the same intimidating manner. There is an inflection they all use when asking for your phone number that implies it to be the most natural part of the transaction. How could anyone have a problem with it?

"That'll be $6.89, please. And what's your phone number, sir?"

"I'm sorry," you say politely, "I'm not comfortable giving that out."

"Why not?" the cashier asks incredulously and with enough volume to let the whole line know that you are a trouble-maker. "I assure you; we keep it in the strictest confidence."

"And I assure you; so do I. Just give me my dandruff shampoo and wart remover. I'm in a hurry."

Refusing to give out your phone number can ruin even the nicest cashier-customer relationships. They can be all engaging and eager to help throughout the process up until that moment of truth.

"How are you today? Did you find everything all right? Some weather we're having, huh? How about those Red Sox? What's your phone number, please?"

Everything is going well; right up until you rebuff him on the phone number deal. Once he realizes you're not going to budge he just gives you a dumb, blank stare for a couple of seconds. The remaining awkward moments of the transaction are wordless and glum. You've tossed all chances of getting a, "Have a nice day," right out the window.

Direct refusals don't send an appropriate message. If you are as tired of giving out your phone number to cashiers as I am, here are some suggestions for appropriate responses. Try one of these the next time a cashier wants your phone number.

• I can't give that out according to the rules of the witness protection program.

• You want my phone number? What's wrong with yours?

• Why should I give you my phone number? You'll never call. You're just like all the rest of them!

• My number is 867-5309. Jenny, I got your number, I need to make you mine.

• Well, umm...my number is 5985479305, but I can't remember the correct order. If you can figure it out, give me a call. It would be a really big help, actually.

- What's a phone number?

There is also of course the option of a preemptive strike. Before the cashier has a chance to ask for your phone number, ask for his. Tell him that you want to send him your catalogue. If he doesn't want to give you his phone number, ask him to explain why.

Don't forget to make him look like a jerk and a trouble-maker to the rest of the people in line for refusing to share his phone number.

Awkward Moments

I'm a big fan of awkward situations. I love to see how people react to them.

For instance, no matter where I go (movies, restaurants, museums, wherever) I always ask for a senior citizen discount, even though I'm only in my mid-forties.

The trick is to do it with a straight face and not to break no matter what.

The clerk is perplexed and has no idea what his/her next move should be.

"Why is this strange man asking me for a senior citizen discount?" the miniature golf cashier wonders.

Sometimes these various employees give me the discount just to avoid a scene, but I like it when they ask to see my identification. That gives me an opportunity to make up a story about having forgotten it at home and my memory not being what it used to be, yada, yada, yada.

Creating these situations can be a lot of fun. Wanna play?

Start off simple. While in conversation with a co-worker, consistently refer to them by the wrong name. This is especially effective if your co-worker started with the company fairly recently. Keep this up for a week and then come in on Monday with an entirely new, but equally incorrect, name for this same person. This is especially effective if the names that you choose are generally reserved for persons of the opposite gender.

"Excuse me, Janice?" you say. "Have you seen the quarterlies yet?"

"My name is Bob."

"Between you and me; we are going to have to do some pretty fast talking to explain those numbers. Know what I mean there, Jan-baby?"

Is that too subtle for you? Try this next one on for size.

Right around lunchtime, pull someone else's Tupperware out of the office refrigerator and then stand right there in the kitchen eating this other person's lunch.

Ideally, you know exactly who owns this particular Tupperware so that you can start complaining vociferously about how "gross" and "putrid" it is just as they enter the kitchen to retrieve it.

"What in the hell is this crap?" you very nearly yell with your mouth full of it. "Who would eat this dog-mess?"

Timing is everything here – a millisecond after they've managed to process the situation, but before they've decided how exactly to handle it, you dry-heave twice, dump the remainder of the food into the garbage, and then bring the empty Tupperware back to your desk.

Here's a good one for you: have you ever found yourself in the lobby of a building with a crowd of people waiting for an elevator? When the elevator finally arrives everyone always does the same thing. Everyone files onto the elevator, they move to the back of the car and then they turn around to watch the floor-indicator lights.

That is proper elevator etiquette.

Here's what you do.

Make sure you are the last one to enter the elevator and then don't turn around. Continue to face the throng of uncomfortable people and watch them go out of their freakin' minds.

If you are really adventurous, go ahead and try to make eye contact with some of them.

No one will outwardly acknowledge this breach of protocol, but each unfortunate person stuck in that car with you will be absolutely beside themselves with anxiety. They will just stand there frozen with fear, defiantly watching the flashing floor numbers appearing just over your head.

"That guy didn't turn," they will each be screaming silently within their heads. "What is wrong with him? He is not looking at the numbers, what is wrong with him?"

Yeah, that's a lot of fun.

Let's say you don't have an elevator handy; you can still play this game.

Go to the bank on a Friday afternoon and get into the long line, but face the wrong way.

Sure, you are going to look like an idiot at first; no doubt about it, but eventually somebody new is going to come into the bank looking to make a transaction. That unfortunate soul is going to have to make a decision about whether or not he really needs to be there. Maybe he can make that deposit on Monday without bouncing any checks.

The best part is that they don't see you until they are almost right on top of you. They are too busy trying to negotiate that stupid roped-off bank line maze-thing and then all of sudden – BAM – the guy at the end of the line is facing the wrong way staring right at them.

They consider going back, but that would require several laborious twists and turns before they can be free of the roped off area.

Sometimes, after an initial hesitation, they will just submit to the situation and will join you in facing the wrong way. This is a good thing, because then they too will be an unwitting participant in creating anxiety for the next innocent fool to show up.

Maintain your commitment and, by the time you reach a bank teller, the whole line is facing the wrong way.

There is one more game that is tons of fun, but I can't necessarily condone it.

Is there anything more awkward than being in a public restroom and having someone mistakenly burst into your stall? I cannot imagine a more vulnerable and humbling moment. Most people live in fear of just such a moment, which is why the occupant of a stall will often issue a "courtesy cough" as you walk into the restroom – that person wants you to know they are there before any confusion should happen to arise.

So, here's what you do.

Whenever you walk into a public restroom, go ahead and "accidentally" bust in on an occupied stall. If it's locked, kick it open.

There are two equally effective techniques for doing this.

In the first method, you just kick the door in without warning and come straight in with a newspaper under one arm. Your facial expression should change from blank to mortified at the exact moment of eye contact.

"Oh, I am so sorry!" you begin. "I can't believe I just did that; I am sooo embarrassed. Please forgive me…"

Continue standing there inside the stall apologizing up and down, over and over again, while the occupant quietly begs you not to worry about it and to just leave.

Eventually you can begin slowly backing out of the stall. Your next move is to, just as hastily, burst into the next occupied stall and repeat the entire process.

The second way to execute this little prank is to burst through the stall door butt-first and continue backing towards the occupied commode until the terrorized occupant begins screaming.

"I'm in here!!!!!!! I'm in here!!!!!!!!" they scream.

On second thought, you're better off not doing that one.

Religious Cults Get a Bad Rap

Religious cults tend to get a bad rap, when actually; they have a number of very strong attributes.

Generally speaking, cult members are required to cut all ties with friends and family. That may initially sound a bit drastic, but think good and hard about your last fifteen Thanksgiving dinners. Let's face it, there is definitely something to be said for abandoning all ties to your relatives and living in a commune alongside hedonistic women with questionable hygiene habits.

Money is always an issue in everyday life. Don't you sometimes get sick and tired of the hassle of having to decide how to spend all of your money? Why should you be bothered with such things? A good cult will remove all that unnecessary stress by taking all of your cash and income. The cult leader then re-distributes the collective wealth of its members to the entire body, as he sees fit. In this regard, at least, cult practices are nearly identical to the intended policies of most prominent Democrats.

Cult members are truly a thrifty bunch, managing to save a ton of money on health insurance every year with the very logical strategy of relying solely on prayer to defend against all illnesses. Personally, I would also recommend that they wash their hands once in a while, but prayer is good too.

Some cults are fortunate enough to have a bona fide faith healer as a leader. That's a good deal if you can find one of those. The Reverend Jim Jones, founder of the Peoples Temple, for instance, used to cure all sorts of deadly illnesses. During public healing sessions he would reach right through the skin of afflicted persons and pull cancers and other serious illnesses right out of their bodies.

Jones and I were very close back in those days, but we had a bit of a falling out when I innocently pointed out that all of the cancers he removed looked remarkably like raw chicken livers. I was expelled from his inner circle and reduced to performing menial tasks, such as going to the supermarket to buy raw chicken liver.

That guy had a great future ahead of him. Too bad he went and led that mass suicide of more than 900 people.

I will concede that mass suicide is one of the major drawbacks of joining a cult. Evidence suggests that suicide cults have existed for thousands of years, but Jones was a true pioneer and he truly redefined the modern-day version of it in 1979 by convincing his followers to drink grape Kool-Aid laced with cyanide.

It is my understanding, by the way, that the fine folks at the Kool-Aid company never endorsed using their product in such a way. While 900 servings undoubtedly represented a substantial sale of their product, the Kool-Aid people would much prefer seeing a smaller volume of sales going to "repeat" customers.

The Heaven's Gate cult certainly took the mass suicide concept to another level in 1997 when 39 of its members determined that a ritualistic suicide was the best way to hitch a ride on the UFO that happened to be following the Hale-Bopp Comet. Heaven's Gate members were rather snobbish and would never have stooped to the Jonestown method of ladling deadly doses of Kool-Aid out of 50-gallon drums and into paper cups. No way. They wouldn't be caught dead doing anything so crass.

The Heaven's Gate members ate single serving sizes of very tasty pudding mixed with lethal amounts of the sedative Phenobarbital and then chased it down with vodka. I'm not sure which brand of vodka was used on that fateful day, but one can bet that it was top shelf stuff – maybe French.

Most of the Heaven's Gate members had a crisp $5 bill and some quarters in their pockets. One can only surmise that the spaceship had a cover charge to get in and had a laundromat or videogame arcade on board. As a very special bonus, they all got a brand-new pair of Nike sneakers to make the trip in.

In retrospect, the whole Heaven's Gate thing seems an awful lot like one of those all-inclusive vacation package deals gone wrong. You know those deals in which a set dollar figure covers the entire vacation – even the food and booze? What a bummer that would be – for your very last earthly thought to be, "Spaceship? I thought we were going to the Cayman Islands."

Luckily for me, I split with the Heaven's Gate movement in late 1996. The basic tenet of their belief, of course, was that a spaceship would deliver the devout to heaven. Well sure, we all believe that, but it was my assertion that any spaceship worth boarding would not mind scheduling a stop on Earth in order to accommodate our entering in a more conventional fashion.

Alas, I was labeled a heretic and was ejected from the group. To add insult to injury, I did not get any sneakers at all – I would have settled for a pair of Converse Chuck Taylors.

The Reverend Sun Myung Moon's Unification Church practices, what many divorced men might consider to be a far subtler form of suicide, in the form of marriage.

The "Moonies" have been around for decades, believing wholeheartedly Moon's assertion that at the age of 15 he was visited by Jesus who implored him to complete the mission he had started. Interestingly enough, it was in 2003 that Moon made an announcement that representatives of the five major religions, along with a contingency of several dozen deceased United States presidents, communicated with him from the Spirit World for the purpose of declaring him as "the Savior and Messiah of humanity."

In 1984, incidentally, the "Savior" did spend some time in a federal prison for tax evasion, proving for once and for all that the IRS is afraid of no one - not even divine deities.

With Moon being the world's savior and all, it is not at all surprising that the only way into heaven is with his explicit blessing – kind of like a Hall Pass to give to St. Peter, I guess.

Moon refuses, however, to provide that vaunted blessing onto unmarried people, which leads to his holding the distinguished honor of being the only messiah of any recognized religious movement in history to appear in the Guinness Book of World Records. You'd have thought the whole loaves and fishes thing would have garnered recognition by the Guinness Book people, but apparently not.

Moon's mass weddings started out modestly enough when he simultaneously married three couples in 1960. He began working his way up and in ten short years he was really rolling, marrying 777 couples in a January 1970 ceremony and another 777 couples in an October 1970 ceremony. Moon reached a pinnacle in February 2000 by marrying 20,000 couples at once. Who would have thought that anyone could have possibly gathered 40,000 of the stupidest people on Earth in one location like that? The logistics of it are mind-boggling. Maybe he really is the savior.

Great Expectations

Parents have such high hopes for their children, don't they?

Everybody's kid is going to grow up to find a cure for cancer or become a professional athlete, and every little thing the kid happens to do is translated into indisputable evidence to that effect.

Most parents don't even wait for the birth before tracking the career path of the child. It starts in utero with the proud father's hand resting on the distended belly of the mother, feeling the baby kick. Invariably every father will say nearly the same thing.

"Wow, that kid has got a great boot. I'll bet we have a future NFL Hall of Fame kicker right here."

There is not a father out there that would translate the same kicking scenario into a prediction of his son going on to worldwide fame as the very first male member of the City Music Hall Rockettes. Likewise, no father alive would envision that the feeling of his soon to be born son's strong, healthy kicking in the womb would someday lead to his appearing on an episode of Cops, handcuffed and inebriated in the backseat of a cruiser trying unsuccessfully to kick out the window for escape. Why not? It seems to happen often enough.

Infants love to grab, pull, and squeeze things with their little tiny hands. Even that simple action is somehow twisted into an affirmation of a proclivity for great strength and advanced dexterity in future years.

It would be refreshing to meet a set of parents with somewhat humbler aspirations for their child.

"Check out the way little Cletus squeezes my thumb," says humble dad. "That's great technique for gas pumpin' right there, boy. Why, he'll be working down the Sunoco station in no time."

"Little Larry has an awful temper and he pulls on my hair whenever the little dickens can get his little hands on it," says humble mom. "He's sure to grow up to be an abusive spouse."

Parents regularly dismiss unwavering evidence of average-to-below-average abilities and intelligence. Your 14-year old kid got his head stuck in between the spindles of the railing for the third time in two weeks? If he didn't have such a big brain it wouldn't get stuck, the parents respond.

Parents' expectations can sometimes rise to levels unachievable for any child to live up to. At some point in the life of an unfortunate child born to such parents, the unbridled expectations are replaced by a cataclysmic despair.

Even if the kid is brilliant, chances are he'll end up disappointing those parents. Albert Einstein, for instance, received terrible grades all throughout his scholastic career.

"Why can't you just apply yourself, Albert?" his mom may have lectured. "You're no son of mine!"

By 1900 Einstein was looking for work as a teacher, but finding no success, was willing to take an assistant position. Even that post eluded his grasp and by 1901 he was working as a temporary teacher at the Technical High School in Winterthur, Switzerland.

His parents had likely given up all hope of excellence by that time and it is unlikely that even Einstein's groundbreaking theory of relativity was enough to redeem him in their eyes.

"Yeah, yeah; E=mc squared. That's great, but where's the follow-up, Al?" his father may have demanded. "What are we supposed to do with that equation, Al? When are you actually going to *prove* it? Did you ever think of that? Why do you have to leave everything half finished?"

Sometimes genius is overrated. I am sure the parents of Sir Isaac Newton walked around proud as peacocks.

"Hello, we're the Newtons. Yes, that's right our son is the young man who discovered gravity. Oh, yes, of course we are very, very proud."

Hey, Isaac; I'm not impressed. As if no one else was going to stumble onto it eventually.

Philosophy Explained

What is our purpose for being here on Earth? What is the meaning of life? What is it all for and what is it all about? The human race has been challenged by these mysteries since the dawn of time. It is perhaps just that unquenchable thirst for the ultimate answer that separates the human race from the lesser animals, and also from hillbillies.

One of my high school friends theorized that our entire universe is nothing but a bowl of fruit in a giant's refrigerator. Consequently, on moral grounds, he refused to consume fruits of any kind in any way. He was a great guy and was way ahead of his time, but we sort of lost touch after he came down with the scurvy.

Philosophers throughout history have endeavored to explain existence and its meaning through logical reasoning; often seeking to accomplish that goal by defining the various aspects of nature and by theorizing of an underlying all-encompassing formula or substance that reality is built upon.

My philosophy professor in college was an elderly little guy with closely cropped white hair and thick glasses. For the life of me I can't remember his name and have come to refer to him as Van Helsing due to his rather uncanny resemblance to the actor Edward Van Sloan, who played the part of Van Helsing in the original 1931 Universal Studios' Dracula.

During the first day of class he proved, through a series of logistical sequences, that, even while we sat there in his classroom, we did not exist at all. I was so convinced of my non-existence that I went ahead and maxed-out all my credit cards. I was later persuaded by a series of very unpleasant collection agents that I did, in fact, very much exist.

Van Helsing wasn't big on pleasantries. He power-walked into the classroom right on time every single session and started his lecture before the door even closed behind him. He spoke quickly with a thick Eastern European accent while writing frantically and unintelligibly on the blackboard. I was able to discern very little of what he said and not a word of what he wrote. I didn't walk away from class with a whole lot of notes to study from.

According to Van Helsing, Thales of Miletus is credited as the inventor of Western metaphysics and philosophy. Thales was the first Greek to abandon, at least partially, the tenets of classical mythology in order to seek explanations for the physical world. Thales, in all of his infinite wisdom, taught that "all things are water."

Water? Everything? Good thinking, Thales. How about rocks? How about saltines? Ever try to swallow saltines without something to wash them down? What a crummy philosopher Thales turned out to be. No wonder almost no one has ever heard of him. History does tend to note him more prominently for his skills as an inventor and engineer, which is probably for the best.

My favorite Greek philosopher is Zeno of Elea and his Paradox of Motion in which he proved that motion cannot be truly defined in any way without encountering inconsistencies.

In his theory of bisection, for instance, Zeno proves that it is impossible to reach point B from a starting point of A, because before reaching point B it is necessary to reach the halfway point between the two. Before reaching the halfway point between A and B, it is necessary to reach a point which is halfway to that. Since it takes time to travel any distance and since every distance, measurable or not, can theoretically be cut in half, there exists an infinite number of halfway points and, therefore, an infinite amount of time is required to pass them all.

That is why, by the way, if you ever find yourself in front of the refrigerator, you might as well grab more than one beer, because according to Zeno, there is a good chance you'll never be able to make it all the way back to the fridge again.

When confronted by Van Helsing midway through the term, I attributed my many absences from his class to Zeno's theory of bisection. I would have made it to every single class, I insisted, had it not been for all of those doggone halfway points. He gave me extra credit for that answer.

Perhaps it was Roland Lawrence LaPrise that best answered the question of what "It" is all about as recently as 1949. LaPrise, who shunned the teachings of the classical philosophers; authored the groundbreaking theory of the Hokey-Pokey.

He taught that you put your right foot in, you put your right foot out; you put your right foot in and then you shake it all about. He goes on to advise that you go ahead and do the Hokey-Pokey and turn yourself around before finally concluding that that's what it's all about.

Further teachings of LaPrise involve the left foot, both hands, and various other body parts including the "backside."

Interestingly enough, recent archeological findings have indicated that Thales was working towards the Hokey-Pokey theory during the first quarter of the sixth century B.C., but went instead with the whole water-is-everything theory. Foolish, foolish, Thales.

Dreams and the Dreaming Dreamers Who Dream Them

There are two things that everyone should know about dreams. Firstly, own dreams don't make any sense except to you. Secondly, they are not even remotely interesting to anyone but you.

True though that may be, it doesn't much matter; people in general have an innate compulsion to relate their dreams to others.

You wake up in the middle of the night with the dream fresh in your head and, just before drifting back off into a peaceful slumber, decide that it is imperative to share this fascinating dream with everybody you've ever met.

The next morning you can't wait to share the dream with your spouse.

"I had the weirdest dream last night," you shout over the Snap, Crackle, and Pop of the Rice Krispies.

"Really? Was I in it?"

That is always the listener's initial question and let's face it; the correct answer is the only possible way to hold their attention. Once we know we're not involved, our interest level falls down to just about zero. Our mind wanders aimlessly while the scattered details of the dream are spouted off in our general direction. Sure, we offer occasional compulsory responses, but we're really just thinking about pancakes.

"Uh-huh," the unwilling listener says. "And that's when the giant panda came in the house demanding orange juice?"

The major problem in verbalizing dreams is that all of the details that made so much sense during the dream virtually evaporate during their journey from the mind to the mouth.

"So then, Marvin Hagler, a really young Chevy Chase, and I were sitting in my uncle's living room…but my uncle wasn't there…and somehow it was my living room…and for some reason I knew that I couldn't eat Jello…"

Regardless, we stubbornly push on with trying to articulate the dream, even though we suddenly realize that the climax is going to be a real let down for everyone.

"And then we all did the Macarena dance even though the Beatles' 'Lucy in the Sky With Diamonds' was playing!" we exclaim to an unimpressed audience. "Is that weird or what? Did I mention that our pockets were full of salsa?"

According to Sigmund Freud, everything in a dream has meaning. I don't buy that at all. Why, then, did I dream of a giant red piano being played brilliantly by the Jolly Green Giant?

Freud was a brilliant man, but he was also a bona fide pervert on a scale with Hustler magazine founder, Larry Flint. Freud deciphering the human mind is akin to Jeffrey Dahmer teaching a course on How to Win Friends and Influence People.

Example? Nearly everybody in the world has had dreams in which they are falling from a great height. According to Freud, a falling dream indicates that you are contemplating giving in to a naughty impulse or urge. Give me a break. Hey Siggy, take off the lingerie and relax a little bit, willya?

It is a fact, by the way, that if you don't wake up from a falling dream before hitting the ground, you die. It

● ● ●

happened to my uncle Snyder. According to the police report, he was sound asleep and yelling, "I'm falling, I'm falling!"

Greatly annoyed by all the noise, my aunt picked him up out of bed and threw him out the thirty-second floor window. He hit the ground before waking up and died right there.

Most adults have some variation of the classic high school dream.

I have a good friend who experiences a reccurring high school dream in which he is taking a test, but is completely unprepared for it. This particular friend failed most of the tests he took while in high school, so his particular variation is really not much of a stretch. He wakes up from this dream covered in sweat and then goes to his job as a Greeter for Wal-Mart.

In my high school dream, there I am, back in high school. It's the middle of the school day and I'm wandering around the hallways, because for the life of me, I can't remember my schedule of classes. I'm completely panicked and peering into the classrooms for an empty desk or possibly a familiar face – anything that might indicate where I'm supposed to be. To make matters worse; I've apparently forgotten to get dressed that day. I'm roaming the hallways completely naked hoping no one will notice.

I'm relieved that nobody in the dream does notice my lack of clothes, but now that I think of it, perhaps I should find that fact in itself to be a bit troubling.

Apparently, a dream in which your teeth are falling out is one of the most prevalent dreams that people experience. Such dreams often include having your teeth falling out one by one for no apparent reason or even crumbling right in your hands.

I've never experienced a dream like that, but my grandfather used to have those dreams nearly every time I stole his dentures.

Nightmares are the worst. We've all had legitimately chilling nightmares, but we've also been terrified by nightmares that, when re-visited, just aren't very frightening.

"There was this white button-down shirt in my dream," you tell your friend. "It had just been cleaned and pressed with light starch and it was on a hanger. Everywhere I went, this shirt would menace me."

"The clean shirt would menace you?"

"Yes. I would see it on the other side of the restaurant while eating lunch. It was lying in the back seat of my car, so I didn't get in. Then, oh Lord help me, it chased me down the hallway at work," you blubber.

"How did the dream end?" your friend wants to know.

"I don't know. Before the shirt could catch me, I woke up right in the middle of my history class. I tried to tell my history teacher about my dream, but he didn't listen. I can't really blame him though, because I happened to be naked at the time."

Mechanical
Resonance

As a kid, I was assigned certain jobs by my parents, but they were never the cool jobs.

My father has always been very talented mechanically. According to my uncles, he rebuilt a Ford big block engine at the age of 4. My father, a humble man, insists that he was nearly 6 at the time.

I remember, quite clearly, helping my father out as he worked on my mother's old Buick in the driveway. I am convinced to this day that he hung onto that car just so he could constantly be required to fix it after work.

"What?!" he'd say at dinner. "The Buick won't start again?! I swear I'm going to junk that heap of trash!"

After dinner he'd gather up his tools and his son, and then out to the driveway we'd go.

His favorite part of the entire "fixing the car" process was definitely the swearing.

I grew up under the impression that four-letter words were specific to the automotive industry. I was convinced that the F-bomb was a particular brand of car parts; as in, "I need a new F****** alternator and a new F****** master cylinder."

Well, he never trusted me to rebuild a F****** carburetor or anything cool like that. The only job ever entrusted to me was holding the flashlight.

The truth of the matter is that I never really expected a promotion either, because I wasn't performing the flashlight task very well. Invariably I'd get distracted and end up shining the light on an area that needed no fixing.

"Pay attention. Can't you see where my hands are?" my dad would ask impatiently. "Well, then shine the light on my hands! What's wrong with you?"

Once in a while I'd be trusted with the responsibility of handing him a wrench out of the tool box, but nine times out of ten, I'd even screw that up by handing him a 3/8 when he asked for a 3/4. Then it was right back to flashlight duty for me.

Now, as a result, I'm basically useless when it comes to automotive repair.

If my car should break down, my only option is to open up the hood and shine a flashlight on it. If that doesn't fix the problem, I'm plumb outta luck.

My father built a shed in the backyard. I remember it like it was yesterday. I didn't get to hammer any nails. I didn't get to stand on the ladder. My suggestion that we add a second floor for the purpose of a secret fort was summarily dismissed. My services were needed only to run to the workshop in the cellar for various tools.

"Go get me the level," my dad said.

Eager to prove my worth, I dashed down to the cellar. I was standing there in the cellar out of breath and scanning through the toolbox before it occurred to me that I hadn't the slightest idea what in the heck a level was.

I didn't want to come back out empty handed, so I grabbed him a beer out of the fridge. He was never really much of a beer drinker, but he was a good dad. He accepted the beer so as not to hurt my feelings, even though it was only about 9:00 a.m., and patiently explained what a level was and what it was used for. I'm still not sure I really understand.

"Steve, go grab me the tape measure," Dad said.

Down to the cellar I dashed, returning five or ten minutes later with another beer.

We continued this process pretty much all day. I had to convince my mother to drive me to the liquor store twice.

I found out a lot about my dad that day. He has an awful lot of patience and one hell of an impressive liver. If you drive by that house today, you will see one incredibly funky-looking shed.

Some things never change.

My father came over my house the other day to help me tune up the snow blower for the winter. We had the snow blower out in the backyard and I must have been sent running into my own house for different sized wrenches on at least three separate occasions before I realized what was happening.

I put a stop to that nonsense immediately.

"This is my house," I told the old man. "You go get the stupid 5/8's."

He did as he was told and I stubbornly took over the actual repairs. It didn't go all that well; mostly, I believe, because my flashlight was broken.

Finally, I had had enough and sent my father into the house for the sledge hammer. It was time, I decided, to just put the thing out of its misery.

He came out of the house with a beer.

I'm hoping it doesn't snow this year, because I can't seem to get the thing started and I've got a whole bunch of extra parts strewn about my backyard.

Jeff Ate a Worm for Five Bucks

We had been there for at least fifteen minutes and had not received the slightest nibble. We were "serious" fishermen, so naturally we were starting to get discouraged.

From where we were sitting we couldn't see much of the surrounding terrain and very little of the pond itself for that matter. Jeff assured me, however, that he had fished here before and this was the best area to set up operations. It did seem to be the only spot where the ground was solid enough this close to the water. The rest of the perimeter seemed to alternate between mud and swamp.

We seemed to be far from civilization, but the nearest house was a very short walk. The road was out of sight due to a hill. We certainly heard every car that passed, but were more or less hidden from view.

It was a beautiful spring day, made especially for guzzling beer and for fishing. We had arrived in style via my new car – a 1975 Chevy Malibu Classic with more rust than paint. It had a vinyl half-landau roof at one point in time, but now it was reduced to the underlying cotton. It had a monster under the hood – a 250 cubic inch straight six with a one-barrel carburetor. When I punched the accelerator to the floor, I could reach 55-miles per hour in about 15 minutes.

There we were; no bites. Jeff suggested that it might be a good time for lunch. I opened up the cooler and took out my chicken salad sandwich and a fresh Miller Lite (no judgements; we were young). I tossed my empty beer can into the brown paper bag so as not to attract attention.

We began eating with the same grubby fingers that had been handling live worms and rusty hooks moments before.

Jeff was three bites into his seafood salad sandwich, an appropriate choice considering the day's event, when I spied his bobber dunking in and out of the water. A sure sign to an experienced sportsman that some sort of aquatic creature is foolishly accepting the bait as a free meal. How superior we were to have fooled this beast. It was time to reel in the prize.

"Jeff, you have a bite," I said.

Jeff spun his head around. Without a moment's hesitation, he dropped his sandwich and grabbed his pole. He began to reel it in, and was faced with quite a fight. More of a fight, in fact, than seemed necessary from my point of view, but I gave him the benefit of the doubt as he roared, "Wow, I've really got a big one here."

And, sure enough, he pulled in a monstrous 5-inch sunfish.

"Well, it seemed bigger under water," he said with conviction.

He glanced over to see whether I was buying into his explanation. I just shrugged and grabbed another beer.

Jeff removed the hook from the fish's mouth and threw the poor thing back. We watched it eagerly swim away. Then Jeff conscientiously wiped the fish saliva and blood off his hands and onto his pants, picked his sandwich up out of the dirt, brushed it off and resumed eating.

I believe it was the combination of hot sun and warm beer that led to the event that has since become known as "The Worm Incident."

I was watching Jeff clumsily baiting his hook when I conjured up a perfect image. I pulled my wallet out of my back pocket and pulled out a crisp five-dollar bill. I held it teasingly in front of Jeff's face.

"I'll give you five dollars if you eat that worm," I dared him.

The worm he had gripped between thumb and forefinger was a beauty; big and fat. Without batting an eye, he threw his head back and held the worm over his open mouth.

Being afraid that I was about to lose my money too easily, I grabbed his arm.

"You have to chew it," I told him.

That didn't faze him in the least. He popped the worm into his mouth and chewed hungrily; with audible crunching noises accompanying each chomp. Finally, he swallowed with a gulp.

I gave him the five dollars. Hell, I would have given him ten.

Peaceful Reflections

Fall is probably my favorite time of the year. It's just perfect for sitting in the peace and quiet of the backyard with a cup of hot coffee. Sometimes I can sit there for hours; especially if I've got Gran Marnier in the coffee.

Sunday was such a day. I was able to sit back, sip my coffee, enjoy the beautiful weather, and allow random thoughts and reflections to wash over me. It has been during just such peaceful contemplative moments in history that some of the greatest mysteries of the universe have been solved.

There in my backyard I began thinking about a poem by Joyce Kilmer. Kilmer once wrote that only God can make a tree. True enough, but just once, I'd really like to see Him make a pitcher of frozen margaritas. It seems like it's always up to me.

While on my second cup of coffee, I began thinking; if I was ever in a situation where I was going to be crossing a desert on foot with a large group of people and I was given a choice of bringing only a canteen full of water or a bag full of beef jerky, I would definitely go for the beef jerky. Sure, I could choose the water, but then I'd be just like everyone else. About halfway across the desert I'd be munching happily on my beef jerky and everyone else would be asking for a piece and I could tell them to go pound sand.

By cup number three, I began recalling my childhood. My friends and I used to play war. We were so naïve about the realities and the atrocities of war. This may have been due to our tender ages, but I think it was really because we were always pretending to be GI's on R & R weekend passes, spending money on women and booze.

By cup number four, I was no longer out in my backyard by choice. My wife had locked me out of the house.

It occurred to me then, that if you're ever going to learn to skateboard, you might as well do it naked. That way you won't rip your clothing.

While sipping on cup number five I was unable to keep the injustices of the world from seeping into my thoughts.

For instance, it sure is tough for a hunchback to get a good job in Hollywood these days.

It wasn't always like that. Back in the 30's and 40's an industrious hunchback was never out of work and practically anchored any self-respecting monster movie. The Frankenstein monster would never have been built if not for that enterprising young hunchback, Fritz. Fritz was an outstanding hunchback with limitless potential and I think it was only his name that held him back from true greatness. Let's face it, if you were a hunchback named Igor back in the day, your chances for steady work more than tripled.

The king of all hunchbacks of course, was good old Quasimodo, the famed Hunchback of Notre Dame. He, and he alone amongst all of the Hollywood hunchbacks, was able to exhibit enough crossover appeal to land a leading-man role. Aside from Quasimodo, hunchbacks generally played second fiddle to some variation of the stereotypical mad scientist that they referred to as "Master." But at least they had a good paycheck and the respect of the industry.

Not anymore. Things are really rough for hunchbacks these days. Not a whole lot of mad scientists out there anymore I guess.

I'd like to employ a hunchback. My hunchback would live in a little house at the foot of my driveway and would be on-call 24/7 for running errands and sending faxes and stuff.

In the winter he would shovel the driveway and in the spring and summer he would blow the sand off of the driveway. In the fall he rakes the whole yard.

A lot of the time he could just sit in front of his little house with his feet up enjoying life, but every morning on my way to work I would stop at his little house and order a coffee. He would have it ready for me and would also provide me with a complimentary newspaper. He would say, "Have a good day at the office, Mr. Bjork," and I would ask him how everything is going and talk about the weather a little bit. Then I would ask him how his wife and kids are and he would tell me that he doesn't have any because he is a hunchback who lives in a little house at the end of my driveway 24/7.

Part Two: Tales from the Road

Beware Bartenders
Bearing Everclear

No, I do not suffer from stage fright – not anymore.

The first time I stepped up to a microphone in a real comedy club was in 1987 at the legendary, original Stitches Comedy Club on Commonwealth Avenue in Boston.

I don't remember the actual date, but it was a Sunday; the night Stitches had perennially allocated for the amateurs, and universally known throughout the industry as Open Mic Night.

I didn't have much fun that night, and it took three years before I dared step back up on a stage. According to the several friends I had in the audience, I did fine – got a couple of laughs. But I was unprepared for the blinding stage lights, and I wasn't aware that is perfectly acceptable not to 'kill' your first time out. I walked off-stage dejected.

I had dreamed of being a comedian since the first time I heard a Bill Cosby album at the age of 7. My mother brought the album home one day because the cover had a drawing of Fat Albert and the Cosby kids. It was entitled "When I Was a Kid" and she didn't necessarily know that it was a recording of one of his stand-up acts. It was the funniest stuff I had ever heard and I wanted to know more about it.

"What does this guy do for a job?" I asked.

"This is it," my mother told me. "He makes people laugh."

"And there's no heavy lifting involved?" I asked. "That's the job for me."

During high school, I made every effort to get on stage as much as possible.

● ● ●

The only production being done in my freshman year was the musical "Oklahoma." That presented a potential problem.

I possess not one iota of musical ability. I can't even play a jukebox.

I was undaunted by this handicap and went for a part anyway. Fortunately for me, they didn't have enough students to fill all the parts – no auditions necessary. I was in.

We were two days into rehearsals when it was decided that, while everyone else sung their lines, it might be best for all involved if I just went ahead and spoke mine.

The production was excellent. We actors were dressed in old western clothes with straw hats and everyone was singing about the tremendous beauty possessed by the great state of Oklahoma with impressive ranges of falsettos and baritones. I lip synched along as the talented people sang:

"Brand new state. Brand new state gonna treat you great!" everyone, but I, sang out proudly.

Things were going well. Everyone sounded great. The audience was smiling.

"Gonna give you barley, wheat, and pertaters," sang a young man.

"Pasture fer your cattle, and spinach and termaters," two young men sang in perfect harmony.

My solo was coming soon.

"Flowers on the prairie where the June bugs zoom," a girl sang angelically.

Then it was my turn.

"PLENTY OF AIR AND PLENTY OF ROOM," I shouted at the top of my lungs.

I could see the audience wince. Not only had I spoken/screamed my lines, but I had also rushed through them, creating an uncomfortable silence before the next guy could come in to save the song.

I don't think I can take full responsibility for this, but no more musicals were produced during the remainder of my tenure at Wilmington High.

It was in January of 1990, nearly three years after my initial plunge, that I stepped back on a stage; this time at Nick's Comedy Stop. It went fairly well, and my expectations were now more realistic. I kept going back, eventually working my way into the ranks of Boston's professional comedians.

I've been on stage thousands of times since then in hundreds of cities, but I'll never forget South Bend, Indiana.

It was 1992 and I was on a tour originating out of Louisville, Kentucky called "The Comedy Caravan." It was a three-week string of one-night gigs in bars located in Kentucky, Ohio, Indiana, and Michigan.

A night in South Bend, Indiana had very recently been added to the tour and the booking agent wasn't entirely familiar with the venue by the time we got there. The bar itself was situated in a nondescript strip mall and looked, from the outside anyway, like it should have been occupied by a video store (when they still existed) or a GNC. The inside was much bigger than one would expect and it sported a décor resembling Saigon circa 1974. Exposed brick was - and still is - fashionable. Exposed cinder block, however, has yet to come into style.

They must have really liked the cinder block look, because they had tossed a couple of broken and crumbling ones on the back of the unpainted plywood stage. The audience, of a hundred and fifty or so, sat in groups of 8 or 10 at round banquet tables.

It was legal, at that time at any rate, in Indiana to serve Everclear. Everclear is 190-proof grain alcohol. For comparison sake, typical vodkas are 80-proof, as are most tequilas.

The front table at the show was jam-packed with 12 Notre Dame students; each one doing shots of straight Everclear and chasing with beer. Most of them were not sure where exactly they were, but they seemed to be enjoying the first comedian.

The bar served the shots in little plastic cups, which looked suspiciously like the ones that come with NyQuil cold medicine. I could see the logic in that - Everclear probably doesn't mix very well with breakable glass shot-glasses.

I couldn't have been on stage for more than five minutes when one of Notre Dame's finest students of the day, who could very possibly be a doctor or a lawyer today, came up with the brilliant idea of doing flaming shots.

Out of the corner of my eye I saw a droopy-eyed-polo-shirt-wearing-malcontent flick his Bic lighter with a smirk and bring it down to his drink. The alcohol caught fire immediately and the plastic shot-glass melted into nothingness, providing the flaming liquid with access to spread out over the entire table. Within a nanosecond the flames had engulfed the other 11 shots, and 12-inch tall flames remained trapped on the top of the table searching for a new source of fuel.

I stood on stage, momentarily at a loss.

The students' instinct for self-preservation had kicked in and they had backed all of a foot-and-a -half away from the table and stared at the flames. The rest of the crowd didn't move and in that instant, which seemed to last for hours, I wondered if it was up to me to get everyone into an orderly single-file line – last one out close the windows – or what?

Meanwhile the largely disinterested bartender casually hopped over his bar, grabbed the fire extinguisher and PHHHHHOOOOOSSSHHH - - took care of the fire.

Everclear must burn very clean, because I really don't remember any smoke at all and I can't recall any lingering odor. I just remember the foam of the extinguisher, which seemed to become powder at the moment of its release.

We were all stunned by the mind-bending events of the last three seconds. No one said a word and no one moved for the next couple of moments, except for the bartender.

I looked down on him from the stage as he methodically replaced all of their Everclear shots, free of charge. He held out his hand and the original pyro dejectedly placed his lighter in the bartender's palm, which signaled each of the foam covered college students to dive back in.

I looked at my watch, which also had a healthy spattering of extinguisher excretion on it, to find that I still had to fill another 25 minutes before I could get off the stage. There was no bailing out – I wanted to get paid.

Straight material wasn't going to work after an experience of that sort. No joke starting with a phrase even remotely similar to, "Have you ever noticed that..." or "Women and men sure are different because..." was going to suffice after a communal experience like the one shared that evening. I had no choice but to spend the remainder of my time on stage ad-libbing about what had just happened.

People always ask if I get nervous before going on stage. I nearly always think back to that fateful night in South Bend, Indiana and answer, honestly, "No, not really. Everclear is not legal in this state."

York, Nebraska

Insanity is not limited to big cities. Every little town in the United States has at least one crazy person. York, Nebraska has one. I met her during the winter of 1993.

At the time, I had been booked for a month and a half at various comedy clubs in the Midwest. I had a couple of nights off due to the holiday, but I was heading for my next engagement in Omaha. I decided to make an overnight pit stop in the entertainment Mecca of York, Nebraska.

Spending ten or twelve hours a day in a small maroon sports car screaming down the freeways of the Midwest makes you long for the next motel room. No matter how cool you keep the vehicle, an unavoidable car-sweat forms slowly over the hours bonding clothes to skin. The smell of stale fast food permeates the car and begins to adhere to your clothing, or more likely, your skin. Soft drinks watered down by melted ice soak through wax-paper cups creating small sticky puddles in the cup holders. The floor on the passenger side is piled high with Styrofoam coffee cups and empty No-Doz packages.

After so many hours of blasting the car stereo, I had trouble hearing the motel clerk and he had to repeat himself more than once. That coupled with the road-worn bright red color of my eyes made the clerk more than a little suspicious of this young stranger who had pulled off the highway and into little York.

He charged me a healthy deposit which, he assured me, would be refunded at check out. Didn't matter to me. All I wanted was a cool shower and a lumpy bed.

* * *

I had only slept for about an hour when I found myself wide-awake again. I was by no means rested, but my internal clock was completely out of whack from the last couple of weeks on the road. I needed food.

It was sometime between two and four in the morning and I was dining in a Denny's, because I value quality. There was only one other patron; a woman eating alone two tables away. On her table were a carton of Camel cigarettes and a box of Hostess donuts. Her coffee was Denny's.

I ordered my breakfast.

Breakfast, by the way, is best eaten at night. Late at night so all the calories and cholesterol have a chance to soak in and relax while you sleep.

A bacon and cheese omelet with a large grapefruit juice and a side of bacon. I like to consume as much saturated fat as humanly possible. The meal comes with toast and a side of hash browns, so we had the starches covered nicely. Coffee is a given. There simply is no real breakfast without a cup of strong coffee. When I say strong, I'm hoping for a two-day-old strong cup of coffee.

I was thoroughly enjoying my meal when this psychotic woman began screaming, "Stop it, stop it, stop it!" to the empty chair across from her.

Then she looked at me and asked me to tell her friend to stop stirring his coffee. Okay, I was game.

"I think your coffee is mixed," I told her imaginary friend. "You can stop stirring it now."

"Ha!" she shouted at the empty chair. "He sure put you in your place."

I was happy to have ended a dispute and dove back into my meal.

Moments later I overheard the lady whispering to her friend.

"He is not a jerk. He's a nice guy," she was saying.

I was stunned. I put down my fork.

"Excuse me," I said. "Did he call me a jerk?" She looked over at me and giggled.

"You're gonna get it now," she told the nothing sitting across from her. I was infuriated. No fictional character calls me names like that!

"Did he just call me a jerk?!" I demanded.

"Yes, he did! He did! He called you a big one!"

I leapt out of my chair, raced over and knocked her friend's chair over. I kicked repeatedly at where his ribs would have been, had he existed. Then I jumped on top of him, hammering the floor with my fists. My nemesis and I rolled around the floor for some time.

"Stop! You'll kill him!" the lady screamed. The next thing I knew she was dragging me off of her buddy.

"That'll teach him," I said while rubbing my lip as if he did manage to get at least one good shot in.

I strolled back to my table in triumph, fixing my shirt and fixing my hair while Madame Psycho crooned over her imaginary Mike Tyson. I sat down and plunged into my feast once again. You can work up quite an appetite stomping on a phantom. The waitress treated me with much more respect after the bout. She looked almost nervous just to be around me. Small town folks can become awestruck quite easily.

The crazy lady ushered her injured friend out of the restaurant and wandered off into the night to who knows where.

From time to time I wonder what has become of her since that night. One thing is certain; these days she thinks twice before acting crazy in front of a perfectly sane person like me.

The Cow Incident

I've had some great times doing comedy on the road. Back when I was single and had no responsibilities, there wasn't much to complain about.

Back then, I drove everywhere. People used to ask why I wouldn't fly to my gigs instead of driving. Flying would have been quicker and the costs would have been about the same after figuring in gas, food, and hotel expenses. But I found it to be nearly a religious experience to be cranking down the highway through the pitch black desolate plains of the Midwest; deranged and wild eyed from a lack of sleep and blasting the music of the Doors at ear shattering levels.

I often kept the windows down to let Morrison scream his "Celebration of the Lizard" at the cows. It was the least I could do. After all, cows can't afford to purchase music and are almost never allowed to listen to the radio.

Don't think for a moment that the cows didn't appreciate my efforts. I was very well liked by the cow populace. Actually, I became somewhat of a cult figure among the cows. I have always understood the plight of the downtrodden every-cow and they could sense that. Over the years I have introduced the Doors to countless numbers of cows. In fact; if you ever see a cow chewing his cud, chances are that he is actually lip synching "Peace Frog."

During that time in my life, to be completely honest, if the Unites States of America ever declared war on cows, I would have had trouble deciding on which side to fight.

I tried to explain all of this to the Indiana State Trooper who pulled me over during the late summer of 1994, but I don't think he understood. He just checked my forehead for a lobotomy scar and sent me on my way. I don't think he has a very good relationship with cows.

He'll pay for his bigotry someday. The cows have his name.

I continued on; performing in such exotic destinations as Springfield and Quincy, Illinois; Cedar Rapids and Sioux City, Iowa for a total of nearly six straight weeks on the road.

The tour went very well until my ride home. All the shows were done and it should have been a straight shot home to Boston. Two or three days max, if I pushed it.

I stopped for some lunch at a nondescript diner located a mile or so off Route 80, just outside of Des Moines. I needed protein and I needed it bad.

I sat down with a good book and a ravenous appetite. I ordered a cheeseburger and fries. I should have known better, but my stomach was doing the thinking for me. The burger was half done and my mouth was full of red meat when I felt it: a presence. I had the distinct feeling that I was being watched.

I glanced around the room, but saw no one eyeing me. Then I looked out the window and saw him.

It was a cow.

I fought back my terror as I tried to conceal what was on the table in front of me, but it was a futile effort. He knew who I was and had seen one of his brothers, half eaten, on my plate.

The cow's first look was one of deep confusion and disappointment. This was quickly replaced with fury as his eyes narrowed. His big cow nostrils flared and he was shaking so hard with rage that the bell around his neck was ringing. Pray that you never see an angry cow. It's a terrifying sight.

The news would spread quickly, no doubt about that. Soon all the cows would know my terrible secret. I would no longer be considered an ally. Indeed, I was nothing less than an enemy now. My life wouldn't be worth spit and let's face it; spit is worth very little.

The cow turned away in disgust and sauntered off. My dread did not subside, however. I know cows. They can be terrible, vengeful creatures. They would not forgive my transgression.

I sat frozen with fear and within five minutes the cow returned with three other cows. They stared at me through the window as I sat with the dreadful evidence lying on my plate. The obvious leader shook her head slowly and then all four turned and walked away. I looked down at my meal. The burger was laughing at me and the ketchup seemed as blood. I jumped out of my chair and upended the table. I screamed, and continued to scream, as I ran from the restaurant; barely hearing the waitress asking, "How was everything today, sir?"

I dashed out to my car and met with a nightmarish sight. My car was perfectly surrounded by fresh, steaming meadow-muffins. I had become a marked man. This was their version of sending me a dead fish in the mail.

I wasn't alone there by the car. I sensed a new and different presence. No doubt about it, a mouth-breather was in close proximity. I snapped my head around and saw him - a teenage boy standing close by. His head was shaved, he had bad teeth, and he was holding a banjo.

"The cows gonna git ya," he told me solemnly.

I jumped in my car and drove off, not looking back. I just kept driving. I passed a field full of cows. They all stopped grazing and looked up at me as I drove by. It was bloodcurdling.

I turned down the Doors and rolled up the windows.

Island of Doom

I've spent the majority of my adult life working as a professional comedian. I use the word "professional," not only because I earned my living that way, but also because I have always made a concerted effort to carry myself in a professional manner. But no one is perfect.

I regret that the names of certain people and places will have to be omitted from this story due to my lack of knowledge relevant to the statute of limitations laws within the state of Massachusetts.

I will concede that one summer night, some years ago, I was booked to work on one of the two small islands off the coast of Cape Cod. I probably shouldn't disclose the name of the island, but it wasn't Nantucket.

The gig was at a club in Edgartown and I was working with two other comedians. We'll call them Jimmy and Mike.

The three of us walked off of the ferry after a calm twenty-five minute boat ride. Enough time to catch up and share stories of recent shows and of life in general. We walked onto the dock past a couple of kids diving for coins - a scene that one might expect to see coming off of a ship onto Jamaica or Haiti, except that these kids were undoubtedly enrolled in private schools and had their own sonar equipment to help find any of the coins that got away.

We soon spied a cabbie holding a sign that said "Comedians." We figured that was probably us.

We drove past sand dunes and tall green grass waving in the warm summer breeze alongside houses, all of the same color. Benjamin Moore, I can assure you, did not get his start anywhere near Cape Cod or the islands. Houses on the Cape are not painted. They are all left au-naturel in order to achieve that gray sea-worn look that Cape Cod is famous for. I had a friend who lived in New Hampshire who tried to achieve that look with his house. He sided it and then refused to paint it in an attempt to get that same Cape Cod look. Whether he used the wrong type of siding, or just wasn't close enough to the sea air, his house just kept getting browner and browner.

"That's just a stage it has to go through," he convinced himself for more than a year and a half. He finally broke down and covered it with paint when his wife was all but out the door.

We arrived at our hotel and checked in. The headliner, Jimmy, got his own room while the opener; which I was, and the middle act shared a room.

It was a nice little club that sat approximately a hundred and fifty people or so, and it was packed to the gills that night.

My act was well-received. I did my allotted twenty minutes and then introduced Mike to an appreciative crowd. Comedians have good nights and bad nights. Sometimes comics blame an audience for a bad show that was entirely our fault, but one can never underestimate the importance of the communal mood of the crowd. A good comedian can usually bring a sluggish crowd around if he's on his game, but a crowd that starts out strong can mean a magic night for a comic. Without exception; the more energy a comedian gets from the crowd the better he is going to perform.

Many comedians, including myself, also enjoy repartee with the audience. Repartee, by the way, is not heckling. A heckle is an aggressive remark made in a competitive spirit.

It has always been my theory that hecklers fancy themselves the funnyman of their group of friends, and that they become envious seeing so many people focusing on someone doing what they had always dreamed of doing, but lacked the courage to try. The heckling is an attempt to massage their ego, even if it means making a fool out of themselves and receiving lifetime's worth of verbal abuse in one night.

Heckling is not fun. It's not generally fun for the comedian – whether he's winning or not - and prolonged heckling is never fun for the audience. Audiences enjoy a jab thrown here and there, but some hecklers, primarily the drunk ones, don't know when to quit. They seem to be convinced that the audience paid a cover charge to see their pitiful attempts at outwitting someone who makes a living at being funny. In those cases, the audiences are robbed of hearing material that the comedian has labored over; material that the comedian has spent countless nights on stage working out the kinks to determine the best wording and the right timing.

I walked from the stage to the bar and ordered a beer and a shot of Cuervo; no salt, no lime. A single shot of Cuervo after a successful show had become a tradition back then when I was a much younger man.

"Hey, I really liked your show," the bartender told me as he put down my drinks.

"Thanks a lot," I replied. I threw down the tequila and chased it with my beer as he watched.

"You really like that stuff, huh?" he asked with a dangerous look in his eye.

"What's not to like?" I shrugged.

He smiled as he walked away.

After the show ended, and the majority of the crowd filed out, I was still at the bar. My friend the bartender was taking good care of me (two more Cuervos, which I hadn't asked for, and several more beers, which I had requested) and I was speaking with a very attractive waitress. Doing very well, I might add.

The bartender came over, grabbed my empty beer glass and stuck it under the tap.

"No thanks. I'm all done," I told him.

He scanned the room and then he assured me, "You're going to need this beer."

How could I argue with that kind of logic?

He put the foaming beer down and told me he had something else for me as he reached under the bar. He came up with a jelly jar filled with, what looked like, cloudy gasoline.

"Try some of this," he suggested.

"What the hell is that?" I demanded.

"It's moonshine," he said, apparently confused by my question. He took another quick look at the jar, apparently to make sure he hadn't grabbed the wrong item.

"No thanks. I don't play with that stuff." It was true – that stuff scared me. People have died from drinking moonshine. The lucky ones just go blind.

"It's not that bad. It's not as bad as tequila. Have one shot," he coaxed as he poured some into a shot glass.

"My friend drinks this stuff whenever he comes in here," the waitress added.

Great. That was all I needed. The waitress had some macho, alcoholic friend that guzzles this garbage like chocolate milk. My male ego had now entered the fray.

I took the glass in hand.

"Why not?" I mumbled as I surveyed my drinking area. My beer was just beside my empty left hand - I would need it the moment this vile liquid was down my throat.

I threw down the shot and chased it. The moonshine immediately evaporated every trace of moisture in my entire body. I became aware of every inch of my esophagus as the moonshine burned sharply all the way down, and then I could feel it land in my stomach with a thud that no liquid should ever make.

"That was horrible," I admitted. I pointed to Mike who was sitting at the other end of the bar talking to a young lady, and paying no attention whatsoever to what was happening at our end. "Give him one of those suckers," I instructed the bartender, who was more than happy to oblige.

He put a shot glass down in front of my friend and poured.

"What's this" the comic asked.

"Steve wants to buy you a shot," the bartender told him.

He took one look at the jelly jar and proved beyond a shadow of a doubt, to anyone who was keeping score, that he was far smarter than I.

"I'll drink that only if Steve does one more."

The shot I had just downed must have started to kick in. Otherwise I have no explanation for why I said, "Okay, set 'em up."

The second shot was not quite like the first. It went down much easier, which was concerning. The first shot of moonshine was undoubtedly already conspiring with the tequila that had already set up operations in my belly. I realized that I had gone too far. I knew that within five to ten minutes I would become a blithering idiot. I didn't want to make a fool out of myself in the club that I had just worked, so I decided to call it a night and go back to my room.

I excused myself, with some difficulty, and walked out the door into the soft cool New England breeze. The hotel was, oddly enough, situated right in the middle of a very quiet residential area, which is probably why the show had to be over by ten o'clock and patrons had to be out of the club no later than eleven. Many parts of Martha's Vineyard turn in early and enjoy quiet evenings, and this was one of those sections. Not at all a good place for a twenty-one-year-old comic bent on moonshine.

The sky was clear, the stars were brilliant and the salt smell from the nearby sea filled my nostrils. The hotel was surrounded on all sides by wealthy homes and was just one property back from the ocean.

The moonshine was really kicking in now and I came up with a new plan – instead of turning in, I decided to head for the beach. A nice walk on the beach with the calming sights and sounds of the waves breaking on the beach might help to sober me up a bit.

It would have been a two-minute walk if I had walked down the lengthy hotel driveway (which ran parallel to the beach), took a right onto the little country road, and followed it down to the beach. A two-minute walk. Two minutes, I reasoned, was far too long to wait. Recalling my high school science teacher's dissertation on the shortest path between any two points, I opted for a straight line, which resulted in my taking a shortcut through someone's back yard. I was very happy with myself as I staggered through this person's private property.

Then I hit the underbrush. It started out light; just tall grass and then it got heavy.

When I got to the thorns it became extremely annoying. That's when I considered turning back, but as I surveyed my surroundings and progress, I decided that I should just push through. It became very dark very quickly as I made my way farther away from the hotel. Occupants of the houses had long since gone to bed and turned out their lights. No need to keep outside lights burning all night in this quiet little neighborhood. I glanced back at the hotel and determined that I had passed the point of no return.

The thorns seemed to go on forever and they just kept getting worse. They started down by my ankles, but eventually started tearing my Levis to shreds all the way up past the knee. I kept going.

My legs were bleeding. I kept going.

I was drunker than I had ever been in my life. I kept on going.

It was pitch black and I couldn't see anything aside from the stars and a hint of a crescent moon. I kept going.

Suddenly, and without warning, there was no more land. I kept going.

I had walked off a cliff.

True, it was a small cliff, but it was a cliff just the same. I ended up free-falling for approximately ten feet before I hit the slope, which forced me into a head-over-heels roll down the embankment and subsequently into a river.

I stood up in the middle of the river, feeling no pain. The water came up to my knees and I was covered from head to toe in mud, seaweed, and gook. It was the dirtiest slimiest river I could have ever dreamed of. If not for the slight current and long narrow appearance, I would have had to describe it as a swamp. Who the hell puts a river this close to a beach?

I wasted a good thirty minutes trying to scale the embankment, which, from water to thorns, stood approximately fifteen to eighteen treacherous feet. I finally became discouraged and took the long way around. I had completely lost interest in walking on the beach and decided it was time to turn in.

On my way back to the hotel I was struck with a brilliant idea. Through the cobwebs in my intoxicated skull I remembered someone telling me earlier that this hotel had a pool. Beautiful. I would just take a quick dip in the pool to clear my head and to clean my body and clothes of all the muck. I had a new mission: Find the pool.

The hotel was made up of one long two-story structure that formed an "L" shape. The club was in the short side of the "L" and the other side was made up of rooms, but the hotel also included a number of small cottages in back of the main structure. It was in a couple of these cottages, as a matter of fact, that we comics were lodged. It was obvious that the pool would be located in amongst those cottages, although it was not immediately apparent where.

I staggered around undeterred for some time before spotting one of the small cottages abutting a large rectangular fence. My intoxicated brain put two and two together and came up with seventeen. I deduced that this building was most certainly the cabana, which would lead to the pool.

I approached the building and opened the door, which, in my defense, was carelessly left unlocked, and then I walked into pitch darkness. From somewhere deep within the dark murkiness I heard snoring.

I had walked into someone's hotel room.

My brain was too fuzzy to immediately recognize this tragic mistake so I just stood there gaping into the darkness trying to see what kind of an idiot would fall asleep in the hotel's cabana. As my eyes began acclimating themselves to the darkness I spied the small college refrigerator on the bureau. That's when I realized how hungry I was.

I lumbered over to the refrigerator and opened it up. The snoring had become little more than comforting background noise that I was barely aware of. My priorities had changed. Inside the refrigerator was a half-pound of sliced ham - perfect.

Somehow, through my stupor, my morals seeped back to the surface and it occurred to me, as I stood there holding someone else's cold cuts, that if I took the ham out of this man's room it would be stealing. I didn't want to steal anything, so I began to eat the ham one slice at a time at the foot of this stranger's bed. He snored; I chewed. Occasionally I glanced over my shoulder at the figure sleeping happily, but I felt not the smallest sense of paranoia as I defiled the sanctuary of his sleeping space. I felt sure that if he woke up he would sit there and listen very calmly to my sad story, after which, he would be more than happy to ration his ham with me.

When there were just three slices left, I decided to be fair to this man who had shared so much with me. I put the three slices of ham back into the refrigerator and noticed that the cellophane was now caked with mud. I saw the mud dripping from the handle of the door of the refrigerator and then the muddy footprints all over the carpeting. Until that moment I had completely forgotten what I looked like. If my gracious host had awakened, he wouldn't have seen anything that resembled a human being.

I slipped out of his room and stumbled back to my own. Not having my key, I was forced to pound on the door until Mike finally woke up to let me in.

He screamed when he saw what was at his door. He was still shaking noticeably when I finally emerged from the shower.

It has been a number of years since my island adventure and I never went back for more moonshine. It didn't exactly hook me in, but I often wonder whatever happened to that jelly jar, and whether it is still being pulled out from beneath that bar.

I'm not proud of that episode, but I admit that every word of it is true, from the first to the last.

I have long since recovered from the thorn inflicted wounds and the cliff inflicted bruises, and even from the dreadful hangover that lasted for more than a day. But somewhere on this Earth lives a frightened shell of a man who has sworn up and down to his friends and family that one moonless summer night on Martha's Vineyard, some kind of swamp monster broke into his hotel room and ate nearly all of his ham.

He doesn't tell the story anymore; he is tired of being mocked, but he feels a strange kinship to those who believe they were abducted by aliens. He knows that there is something not quite human lurking out there in the night, hungering for sliced ham.

● ● ●

I'm willing to bet that he doesn't sleep as well as he once did, and I guarantee that he never sleeps without checking the door lock several times.

There are, by the way, two very important morals to this cautionary tale of bad decisions. Never, never, never drink anything that is served out of a jelly jar, and don't ever go to sleep with your doors unlocked.

You never know when I'll be performing in your hometown.

Acknowledgments

These pages are ostensibly to thank all the people who contributed to this collection. However, since I did pretty much all the work, I fully intend to hog for myself all the credit/criticism/disappointment/disinterest that this book may garner.

Over the course of my life and my career, I have become indebted to many people, and I'd like to use this space to thank them.

My wife, my best friend, Georgett, is most certainly first on my list. She has always encouraged and supported me in every foolish endeavor I've ever engaged (even the brief period that I thought I might like to buy an ice-cream truck). She's the best thing that ever happened to me. I'm grateful every day, and this book is dedicated to her.

I thank my parents, Paul and Kathryn, for being the finest parents anyone could ever ask for. Thanks to them, I grew up in a safe, happy home where I always felt loved and where I learned the value of humor. I thank them for enduring my, no doubt, torturous childhood stand-up routines in the living room.

My kids make everything worthwhile – Michael (no longer a kid), Cheyenne, Blake, Isaiah, and Kari.

My thanks to my sister, Karin, for willing to be the butt of most of my jokes growing up. Karin has the best sense of humor of anyone I know. My mother has always said that Karin was the funnier of her children.

Thank you to Willy Drinkwater. Willy was the General Manager of Stevie D's Comedy Tonight when I first started working there as a doorman during my freshman year of college in 1987. He encouraged me to take that first plunge into stand-up, and continued to encourage me for many years as I developed into a professional. As a young, struggling comedian, he, his wife Yvette, and their sons Ian and Allen became a second family to me. I will never forget, nor will I ever be able to repay, all that they did for me.

I will forever miss the late Steve D'Addario, owner of Stevie D's Comedy Tonight. His club was one of the premiere comedy venues in Boston during the 1980's and early 1990's, and he gave me a shot to take that stage before I had probably earned it. He was a great man and a good friend.

To comedians Jimmy Dunn and Paul D'Angelo – thank you for the early encouragement when I needed it most. Both of them took me under their sizable comedy wings and helped me in so many ways transition from open mic'er to professional.

The Boston Comedy scene is tight-knit and I appreciate the many friends I have in that community. There are far too many to name, but if you're a Boston comedian, and you're not a jerk, I appreciate your friendship. If I start naming names, I'll leave someone out and feel like a heel.

Kevin Knox, Rich Ceisler, and Bob Seibel were true legends in the Boston Comedy scene. They were great people and great friends. They were taken before their time. I miss them.

Comedian and club owner Dick Doherty gave me a ton of stage time in the beginning of my career. He gave me my first paying gig at a comedy club, and was the first booker to use me as a headliner. I thank him and his wife Kathy for many years of friendship.

After I got married, I dropped out of comedy for several years. I owe a big thank you to Dave Rattigan, comedian and booking agent, for helping me transition back into the scene. Not only did he fill my calendar with his gigs, but, on his own initiative, he proactively reached out to other booking agents on my behalf. I will always carry that debt and he will always have my unfailing loyalty.

A special shout-out to comedian Jackie Flynn. In 1995, he and I made a three-week road trip from Boston to Los Angeles. In the midst of that trip, he also arranged for my first performance at the Riviera Hotel in Las Vegas. I will never forget that adventure.

My "long-suffering" editor Shawn Sullivan certainly deserves mention. In 2002, on a whim, I sent a note and a couple of samples to the editor of my local newspaper. I figured it could be a fun little hobby to write some articles for my local paper. He hired me as a freelance reporter, which was tremendous fun. I spent far more hours writing, and subsequently editing, for that little paper than I ever imagined I would. Little did I know that it would lead to such a valued and enduring friendship.

Thank you to Steve Harvey. Though I can't imagine he would ever remember this, we were introduced during my first visit to the L.A. Improv in the mid-1990's. When he was informed that I was new to Los Angeles, he took me aside and spent more than an hour counseling me and advising me about the L.A. Comedy landscape. I'll never forget how generous he was with his time.

Also by STEVE BJORK

Verbs! What Are They Good For? Huh! Absolutely
Nothing! Say It Again!

A Complete Unabridged History of the Hokey Pokey

Rectangles and Other Confusing Shapes

Vomit, In Written Form

Oh, The Places My Belly-Button Lint Has Been

Made in the
USA
Middletown, DE